Making Afghans from Favorite American Quilt Patterns

Making Afghans from Favorite American Quilt Patterns

Valerie Kurita

DOUBLEDAY & COMPANY, INC.
Garden City, New York

*To my family — husband, Frank;
sons, Andrew and Julian; and
daughter, Elizabeth — for their
patience and support*

Library of Congress Cataloging in Publication Data
Kurita, Valerie.
  Making afghans from favorite American quilt patterns.
  1. Afghans (Coverlets) 2. Quilting — United States — Patterns. 3. Knitting — Patterns.
4. Crocheting — Patterns. I. Title.
TT825.K867   1985   746.9'7041   84-26034
ISBN 0-385-18545-6

Every effort has been made to ensure the accuracy and
clarity of the directions in this book. Although we cannot be
responsible for misinterpretation of directions or variations
caused by the individual's working techniques, we would be
happy to answer any questions you may have about the
directions. Address inquiries to the author, in care of Genie
Books, 218 Madison Avenue, New York, NY 10016.

Contents

Preface 6

Introduction 19

About the Book 20

Before You Begin 21

Alternative Uses for Quilt
  Designs 23

Metric Conversion
  Table 24

Abbreviations, Symbols,
  and Terms 25

Knitted Afghans 27

1/ Tree of Life 28

2/ Tulips 31

3/ All-White 34

4/ Joseph's Necktie 37

5/ Goose Tracks 41

6/ Flying Geese 44

7/ Log Cabin 47

8/ Homestead 50

9/ Shoofly 53

10/ Sawtooth 56

Knitted Lap Robes 59

11/ Roman Stripe 60

12/ Baskets 62

13/ Indian Hatchet 66

14/ Double Irish
  Chain 68

Knitted Baby
  Blankets 71

15/ Cats and Mice 72

16/ Baby Blocks 76

17/ Interlocking
  Squares 79

18/ Baby's Nine-Patch . . 81

Crocheted Afghans 85

19/ Wedding Ring 86

20/ Mosaic 88

21/ Lone Ring 93

22/ Bridal Wreath 96

23/ Canopy 98

24/ Rose of Sharon 102

25/ Dresden Plate 106

26/ Grandmother's
  Fan 109

27/ Patchwork Puffs . . . 112

28/ North Carolina
  Lily 115

Crocheted Lap
  Robes 118

29/ Star of Bethlehem . . 119

30/ Zigzag 124

31/ Broken Dishes 126

32/ Storm at Sea 128

Crocheted Baby
  Blankets 131

33/ Yo-yo 132

34/ Clamshell 135

35/ Trip Around the
  World 138

36/ Baby's Flower
  Garden 141

Stitch Glossary 145

A Portfolio of
  Traditional Quilt
  Motifs 153

Acknowledgments and
  Sources 160

An Album of Traditional American Quilts, page 8

Preface

At last, for our many American crocheters and knitters who admire the handmade quilts of yesteryear but who would prefer to work with a crochet hook or knitting needles, here are thirty-six afghan designs interpreted from classic American quilts.

These quilts are valuable to us on several levels. Not only do they record the history of a nation, but each also has a history of its own. Every good quilter knows the background of the quilt he or she is reproducing. Some of this information is given on these pages so that crocheters and knitters using this book may share the feelings of the American frontier women who took this particular art form to new heights, first out of need and later out of the desire to make something beautiful.

American quilts have evolved from basic patchwork to elaborate appliqué and trapunto-like quilted and stuffed masterpieces. The breadth of design variation between these styles includes hundreds of designs now considered worthy of recording and preserving. The approach to quilt making can range from a practical recycling of salvageable parts of clothing and scraps of fabric to detailed and planned designs incorporating large pieces of fabric bought specifically for the quilt.

Fortunately for quilts, America was settled at a time when handicrafts in England had reached a refined stage. The new arrivals in America brought what tools they could. But, more important, the forefathers and foremothers brought their skills, knowledge, and a creative approach to a rather bleak situation, high in hardship and low in worldly goods.

Faced with a shortage of clothing and bedding and an excess of cold winters, the women found that there was not enough fabric of ample size available to make one-piece quilts, so as clothing wore out, any unworn pieces were saved. The larger pieces were used for children's clothing, the smaller saved for quilts. From these small, irregularly shaped scraps was born the patchwork crazy quilt.

Indeed crazy, these first quilts were created with no plan for color arrangement, shape, or materials. As they were acquired, the pieces were fit together puzzle-fashion and joined with needle and thread. Any quilts of this type that have survived have given us the material recording of the fabrics' content and weave typical of the period.

The second stage of the crazy quilt developed as more fabric became available, usually imported from England. The top was then made of blocks rather than irregular shapes, but it remained an unplanned mixture of colors and fabric types. On both the earlier and later crazy quilts, decorative stitches were used, such as the buttonhole and chain stitch. Occasionally, the motif on the fabric was outlined in stitches or a small decoration was embroidered onto a plain patch or block.

(Actually, the term "patchwork" is a misnomer; these quilts were pieced together. "Patch" implies that one piece of fabric is sewn onto another, which is appliqué, a technique used in quilting a few generations later than that of the crazy quilts.)

A more rational approach to quilting followed, called the Roman Stripe, in which light-colored blocks were sewn together in a strip that was, in turn, sewn to a strip of dark-colored blocks. The entire quilt top was constructed of alternating strips of dark and light. From the Roman Stripe evolved the checkerboard Brick Wall: strips of blocks were sewn together so that the seam between two blocks fell at the middle of a block below to give the effect of a brick wall. These early one-piece designs also include the Honeycomb, which is composed of strips of hexagons sewn together and is the forerunner of the Mosaic patterns.

Becoming ever more sophisticated graphically, quilt designs evolved into a two-piece series—squares or rectangles were cut into triangles and then rearranged into complex designs of dark and light. From this series came the diamond and star variations.

A progression of geometric designs evolved from the three-piece design to the Nine-Patch and then to multiple patterns. By adding appliqué to these geometric multiples, quilters could increase the complexity of their patterns to any degree they wished. These kinds of designs accounted for about 90 percent of the quilts made during the late 1700s and the 1800s.

The pinnacle of quilting technique was reached with the one-piece all-white quilts. Elaborate designs were quilted on these and then stuffed. The center medallion was often an urn of flowers and/or fruit or a bouquet, framed with vines or twisted ropes or any one of another dozen popular borders. The background was often quilted in small diamond shapes.

The all-white quilts were the highest level of artful design created by the early American quilters; these needleworkers, like the previous generations of quilters, were inspired by a variety of sources. Women copied or modified stenciled designs on walls, the decoration on their china, and the motifs found on fabric imported from England and France. They stylized versions of plant and animal life, as well as the sun and the stars, and sometimes even the elements—wind, snow, rain.

This book shows crocheters and knitters how to make an afghan born of the history of and evolution in quilt design. This has been made possible thanks to the imaginative interpretation and skill of the designer, Valerie Kurita, an accomplished knitter and crocheter and lover of the art. The group of pages directly following this preface features some of the original quilts from which Ms. Kurita drew her inspiration.

Gail Kahl

An Album of Traditional American Quilts

Presented here are just a few of the quilt designs that inspired the knitted and crocheted afghans in this book.

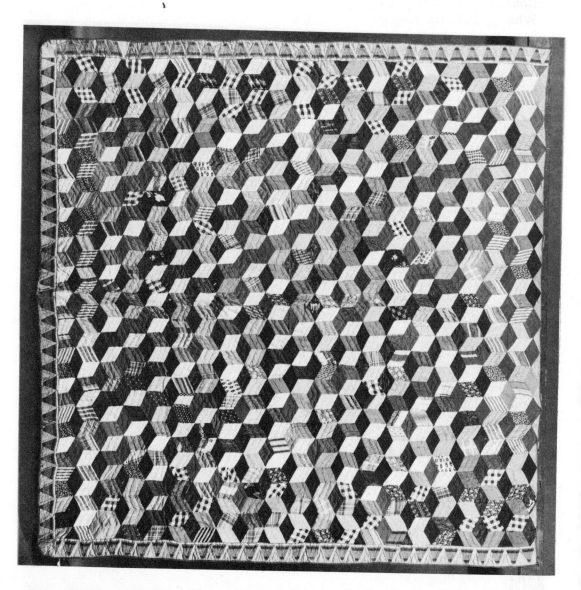

Baby Blocks, or Diamond, Quilt

This Diamond quilt, also called Baby Blocks, was made in 1860. Through the arrangement of dark, light, and medium-toned diamonds, an optical illusion is achieved, making the cubes appear concave and convex at the same time.

Courtesy of the Brooklyn Museum; gift of Mrs. Robert Marian Rogers

Mosaic Quilt

The Mosaic pattern developed out of the Honeycomb design, which is a series of hexagons. Through the sequence of the colors used, dark with light, this Mosaic takes on a floral effect. This quilt was made during the 1880s.

Courtesy of the Brooklyn Museum; gift of Mrs. Mathilda Maxwell Whiting and Mrs. Howard F. Whitney

Log Cabin

Each square in the traditional Log Cabin design is made up of strips that become progressively longer as they are arranged concentrically around a small square. The overall quilt design is achieved through the use of light with dark and the specified placement of each square. This quilt was made during the late 1800s.

Courtesy of the Brooklyn Museum; gift of Mrs. Emmie B. Butler

Tree of Life

The Tree of Life design, originally from the Far East, first appeared in America on fabrics imported from Europe intended as wedding gifts. Symbols of eternity — bud, flower, and fruit — were all growing on the same tree, which was traditionally surrounded by exotic birds, squirrels, monkeys, butterflies, and miniature elephants. For the purpose of quilting, this version was simplified to a stylized tree made up of triangles pieced together into a four-patch pattern. This particular quilt was made during the 1800s.

Courtesy of the Brooklyn Museum; gift of Mr. and Mrs. Gustave Gilbert

Garden Basket

The Garden Basket quilt is a two-patch design. The bottom of the basket is pieced as a one-patch design and the flowers are appliquéd onto the second patch. The two triangular patches make one square of the pattern. This nineteenth-century quilt was probably made by a group of women, each creating her own version, because each square displays a different floral arrangement for the contents of the basket.

Courtesy of the Brooklyn Museum; gift of Mrs. Margaret S. Bedell

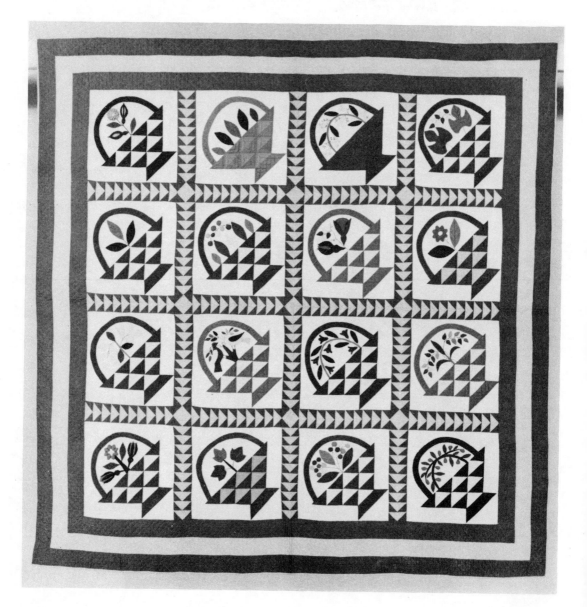

Rose of Sharon

The entire Rose of Sharon design of this quilt is appliquéd onto a solid background. There are many roselike designs called the Rose of Sharon, a name taken from the Bible; however, this quilt incorporates one of the four most popular.

Courtesy of the Brooklyn Museum; gift of Mrs. Margaret S. Bedell

North Carolina Lily

This nine-patch classic has survived for more than a century with very little change, but it has had many names, ranging from Wood's Lily in New England to the Mariposa Lily in California. In Pennsylvania it is called Tulip. This version was made in 1850.

Courtesy of the Brooklyn Museum; gift of Mrs. Margaret S. Bedell

Star of Bethlehem

   Also known as the Lone Star, this example of the Star of Bethlehem quilt was made by the Amish in Pennsylvania. It is constructed of many small diamonds arranged in a four-patch top. Each patch contains two points of the eight-pointed star. This version was made about 1920.

Courtesy of the Brooklyn Museum; anonymous gift

Double Wedding Ring

One of the more intricate designs in quilting, the Double Wedding Ring is also a mathematical achievement. The four-patch motif comes together to form overlapping rings. The rings themselves are made up of small wedges pieced together around a melon shape that is then appliquéd onto a solid background. Perhaps the complexity of the wedding rings was meant to reflect the variety in the married life of the original designer. This version was made in the 1920s.

Courtesy of the Brooklyn Museum; gift of Mrs. Dorothy M. Kitzele

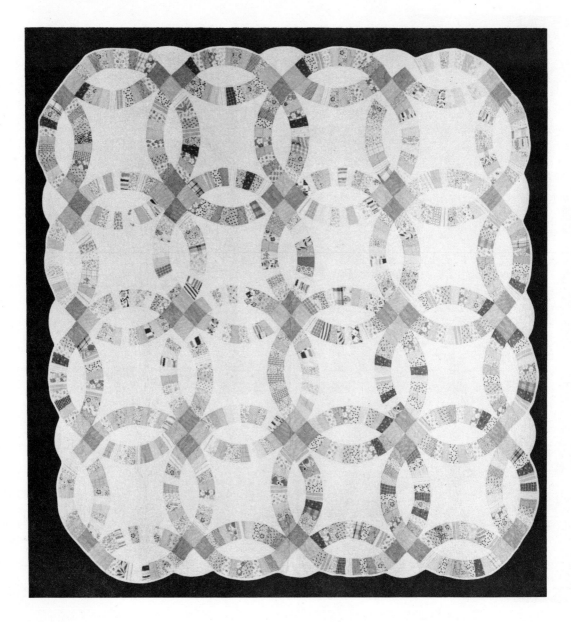

All-White

This embossed all-white quilt is the rarest of all types of quilt. It is usually made of homespun cotton or linen, and the reverse side is often as pretty as the top. Very much like that of Italian trapunto work, the technique involves raising portions of the design by inserting string into stems and scrolls and stuffing flowers and other broad areas with cotton.

Courtesy of the Brooklyn Museum; gift of Mrs. Mary Dunderdale Bedell, Mrs. Maria Dunderdale Dange, and Mrs. Forbes Dunderdale

17

Introduction

I've always admired the beautiful designs of traditional American quilts, appreciating both the country mood that quilts evoke when incorporated into an interior decorating scheme and their capacity to stand on their own as works of folk art equal to needle-art specimens produced by any other culture in the world. In recent years a number of persons with fine-arts backgrounds have entered the field, designing quilts with sophisticated use of color and geometric form. These designs are more often than not turned over to expert quilters to be executed; the quilts then find their way into museums, where they are exhibited as works of modern art.

Though many people feel that knitting and crocheting require great patience and perseverance, I, having knitted and crocheted for many years, am awed by the dedication required to make a quilt — to cut the tiny modules of fabric perfectly, carefully piece them together, and meticulously sew them in place. Not yet finished, the quilt must then be padded, backed, and topstitched with a quilting design, preferably by hand.

Not being an expert seamstress and not having the time required to make a quilt, I have always felt that these traditional quilting motifs were out of my reach until it occurred to me that I could adapt the designs to the crafts I know best and love most — knitting and crocheting.

The results of this thoroughly satisfying endeavor are here for you to re-create in this collection of thirty-six knitted and crocheted afghans, lap robes, and baby blankets, each based on an American quilt design. As knitters and crocheters, we create the fabric for our quilts with needles or hook and yarn, just as some of the pioneer women originally created their fabrics with spindles and looms. After serving other practical purposes, those fabrics finally made their way into the pieced quilts that have been cherished by generations of Americans. Our translation of that pieced work into afghans displays the additional dimension of textured stitches; these knitted and crocheted blankets will doubtless become cherished heirlooms in their own right.

My wish is that this book will be of value to you for a long time and that those of you who begin with the easy knitted Roman Stripe or simple crocheted Zigzag will go on to try the intermediate and advanced projects as you gain skill and confidence. Before you undertake one of the afghan projects, take a few minutes to read the sections that precede the instructions — you'll find them helpful throughout your work.

Valerie Kurita

About the Book

Simplified Instructions

During the fall of 1979 a committee was formed by representatives of the yarn industry and knowledgeable professionals from major consumer publications. This committee developed a simplified instruction system for hand knitters and crocheters. As a result, abbreviations relating to knitting and crocheting and size measurements were accepted by all in a standard form. The system was made available to all publications dealing with knitting or crocheting, both inside and outside the industry, so that the hand-worker would not experience variations in interpretation while using different publications. Wherever the "Simplified Instructions" logo appears in one of those publications (see p. 25), these standards have been followed, as they have been followed throughout this book.

Instructions Format

Each set of instructions begins with an "Approximate Finished Size." To ensure that the finished project measures that size, take the time to work out the required gauge given in the instructions. (See "Before You Begin — to Determine Gauge.")

With each set of instructions is a black-and-white detail photograph to clarify stitches, the arrangement of pieces, and any other elements critical to the project's design.

The yarns used for the projects appearing in this book were generously supplied by a number of yarn companies. Because the projects were designed with these yarns in mind, it is recommended that they be used for accurate results. (See "Sources" for the company addresses.) Under "Materials," the brand name, color number, name of each color, and amount of each yarn required are listed. To substitute a yarn from another manufacturer, refer to the generic yarn type appearing in parentheses (for example, sport weight, knitting worsted weight, bulky weight) and buy yarn of that designation. Be sure to buy the total amount, in weight, specified for the original yarn so that the skeins will be all from the same dye lot. If the name of a color may not be easily understood (many are in French) and may therefore be difficult to substitute for, an explanation is given in parentheses. After you have the yarn, be sure to test the gauge.

Stitch Glossary

Illustrations of all the fundamental knit, crochet, and embroidery stitches used in the projects are given at the back of the book (see "Stitch Glossary") with clearly stated directions. However, they are no substitute for a hands-on teacher. Whenever possible, take advantage of an experienced knitter or crocheter willing to demonstrate unfamiliar stitches to you.

Before You Begin

To Determine Gauge

The gauge is the number of stitches worked per a square-inch measurement, and that depends on the weight of the yarn, the size of the needles or hook, and the amount of tension used. All these determine the texture of the work and the size of the finished piece. Even a small discrepancy in the gauge can result in a large difference in the finished piece; therefore, it is important to make sure that you are working the proper gauge by doing a test piece of at least 4 inches. For example, given a gauge in stockinette stitch of 5 stitches = 1 inch, 7 rows = 1 inch, work the test piece as follows: cast on 20 stitches and work in stockinette stitch for 28 rows. The piece should measure 4 inches square. If it is too small, try larger needles; if too large, use smaller needles; and adjust until the correct gauge is obtained.

To Use Charts

Always start at the bottom of each chart, working the odd-numbered rows from right to left and the even-numbered rows from left to right. Unless otherwise specified, the odd-numbered rows are worked on the right side and the even-numbered rows are worked on the wrong side. Any rows not shown on the chart will have directions given in the step-by-step instructions.

To Work Single-Crocheted Edgings

Occasionally, before components of a project are joined or after a whole afghan has been made, the edges need to be finished with a single-crocheted edging in order for the piece to lie flat. Usually it is up to the crocheter to determine the exact number of stitches necessary.

If you are working along a side edge of a knitted piece, work into a knot rather than a thread whenever possible so that holes won't be created along the finished edge. If you are working across the top or bottom edge of knitting, it is best to skip every third or fourth stitch instead of working into every one, to prevent the edge from rippling. There will be a bit of tension in the edge, but, when blocked, the piece will flatten perfectly. If the piece is a square, be sure that the same number of stitches are worked along each side, with three stitches in each corner.

In some projects, a single-crocheted edging is specified to be worked "color over color," which means that the color of the edging should match that of the edge of the main piece.

To Block

There are some yarns, such as mohair, that, by nature, need no blocking; many of the newer yarns also need none. Whenever blocking is essential to the design, however, it will be called for in the directions. For instance, squares knitted on a diagonal usually come out diamond-shaped; they must be blocked to a square shape before they can be edged and/or joined. In this case, shape the piece as desired, pin it to a padded board, and cover it with a damp towel. Then steam it by holding an iron in contact with the towel, never putting full pressure on the piece but allowing the steam to do the work. Let the pieces dry completely before removing them. When blocking is not stipulated, it is up to you whether to block or not, depending on the yarn type, the appearance of the seams, and the finished look of the project.

To Change Color in Crochet

For a pattern that incorporates two or more colors throughout, there are two ways to change from one color to another: (1) if the colors are used interchangeably throughout, loosely carry along the unused yarns behind the work or work over the unused colors while they lie across the top of the previous row; (2) if colors are worked only in specified areas, wind a separate bobbin for each of those colors and use the ball of yarn for the main color. This will eliminate the need for carrying colors along the work.

In either case, while working across a piece, use the following method to change color. Work the last stitch of the first color up to the last yarn-over drawn 'through, hold the first color to the left, yarn over with the second color, and pull it through the loops on the hook to finish the stitch. Continue working with the second color, carrying the unused yarn as previously explained.

To Change Color in Knitting

If you are working stripes, carry the unused yarn along one edge of the work by twisting it around the yarn in use at the end of each row at that edge.

If many colors are used but they are confined to one area, use bobbins for each color but the main one. When changing colors, twist the two yarns once and then work across, using the second color while carrying the main color loosely across the back of the work by twisting it with the working color every 5 to 8 stitches.

If only two or three colors are being used alternately throughout, carry the unworked colors loosely across the back, twisting them one at a time with the main color every 5 to 8 stitches and twisting at the stitch just before the color change is made.

Alternative Uses for Quilt Designs

Many of the afghan designs included in this book have a repeated motif or motifs that can be used to make a pillow cover or a wall hanging. Any part of a design can be adapted, although a motif that has a square or rectangular shape is easiest.

Once you have chosen a motif, knit or crochet it according to the directions for the afghan from which it has been taken and using recommended or desired yarns. Block the finished work and then single-crochet an edge or border around it (see specific directions below).

Pillow

To make a pillow, you will need a knitted or crocheted pillow front with a crocheted border and in the desired color and size; a pillow form 1/2 inch less all around than the pillow front, or stuffing and muslin to make a pillow form; and fabric for the pillow back.

To make a pillow form, cut two pieces of muslin to the size of the pillow front. Pin the pieces together; stitch a 1/2-inch seam on three sides and, on the fourth side, 1 inch in from each corner, leaving an opening. Clip the corners, turn the form right side out, and stuff it through the opening. Slip-stitch the opening closed, turning under the raw edges.

Cut a piece from the fabric for the pillow back to the same size as the pillow front. Pin the pillow front to the back, right sides together, stitch a 1/2-inch seam around three sides, and leave the fourth side open. Clip the corners on the fabric piece only and turn the pillow covering right side out. Insert the pillow form. Slip-stitch the open side closed, turning under the raw edges.

Small Wall Hanging

To make a small wall hanging, you will need a knitted or crocheted motif, with a crocheted border, in the color of your choice; a frame, including glass and cardboard backing, in a size to accommodate the piece; and thin cardboard.

To frame the motif, cut a piece of the thin cardboard to the size of the backing cardboard that comes with the frame. Run a line of glue along all four edges of the cardboard, center the work over the cardboard, and press its edges into the glue; let the glue dry thoroughly. Insert the work into the frame behind the glass and then slide the cardboard backing into place.

Full-Size Wall Hanging

To make a full-size wall hanging of your afghan, you will need a knitted or crocheted afghan; a piece of duck cloth or canvas 2 inches larger all around than the finished afghan; nylon thread; small upholstery tacks; a dowel measuring the width of the afghan; and two hooks into which the dowel will fit snugly.

To assemble the hanging, turn under 1 inch of the cloth twice all around and topstitch in place. Lay the afghan over the fabric with the afghan right side up and the fabric turnovers also facing up. With needle and thread, baste the afghan to the fabric around all four edges. Then tack the two together in rows 6 inches apart across the entire afghan. Using upholstery tacks, tack the width of the afghan to the dowel, placing the dowel just under the top edge. Insert or attach hooks to the wall, spacing them so that they are one-third the width of the afghan apart, and rest the dowel on the hooks.

METRIC CONVERSION TABLE

Linear Measure:
1 inch = 2.54 centimeters
12 inches = 1 foot = 0.3048 meter
3 feet = 1 yard = 0.9144 meter

Square Measure:
1 square inch = 6.4516 square centimeters
144 square inches = 1 square foot = 929.03 square centimeters
9 square feet = 1 square yard = 0.8361 square meter

ABBREVIATIONS, SYMBOLS, AND TERMS

beg	begin, beginning
CC	contrasting color
ch	chain
ch-	(chain dash) refers to chain or space previously made, e.g., ch-1 sp
dc	double crochet
dec	decrease, decreases, decreased, decreasing
hdc	half double crochet
inc	increase, increases, increased, increasing
k	knit
lp(s)	loop(s)
MC	main color
p	purl
pat(s)	pattern(s)
psso	pass slip stitch(es) over [stitch(es)]
rep	repeat
rnd(s)	round(s)
sc	single crochet
sl st	slip stitch
sp(s)	space(s)
st(s)	stitch(es)
tog	together
tr	triple crochet
yo	yarn over
* or **	These symbols indicate that the directions immediately following are to be repeated a given number of times.
( )	Instructions within parentheses are to be repeated a given number of times.
Work even	Means to work without increasing or decreasing, always keeping pattern as established.

Simplified Instructions

1

Knitted Afghans

1 / Tree of Life

Approximate Finished Size: 49 by 57 inches
Experience Needed

The Tree of Life design is also called the Pine Tree and the Christmas Tree. This familiar motif was originally borrowed from the popular printed cotton fabrics brought to America from Persia and India in the days of the clipper ships. The settlers of the New World were religious, and the stylized tree was, in their minds, linked with their belief in the eternity of life. Traditionally, the Tree of Life is a green-and-white quilt, but here the trees are knitted on a stockinette peach background and framed with solid and checkerboard borders. (See p. 11 for a photograph of a Tree of Life quilt.)

Materials:
Columbia-Minerva Nantuk, 4-ounce balls (knitting worsted weight):
   3 balls color 5704, peach
   3 balls color 5733, medium olive (light green)
   3 balls color 5965, medium sea green (dark green)
   1 ball color 5992, camel
Knitting needles, No. 10, or size required to knit to gauge
Crochet hook, size H
Yarn needle

Gauge in Stockinette Stitch: 4 stitches = 1 inch; 11 rows = 2 inches

Note: To work the stockinette st: K 1 row—right side; p 1 row—wrong side. To work the reverse stockinette st: P 1 row—right side; k 1 row—wrong side. When changing from one color and st section to another, be sure to work the first row of new color so that it appears as a k row on the right side of the work.

Tree of Life Strips: Make 3. With peach, cast on 34 sts. Work in stockinette st, following the 44-row chart for color changes, and rep from A to B four times—176 rows. Bind off.

Border:
Side Strips: Make 2. With medium sea green, cast on 48 sts. Work even, following border chart for st and color changes, and rep from A to B eight times. Bind off.
Top and Bottom Strips: Work as for side strips but rep from A to B six times instead of eight. Bind off.
Corner Squares: Make 4. Cast on 48 sts. Work even in reverse stockinette st for 12 inches. Bind off.

Finishing: Sew the three tree-patterned strips together. Sew the side, top, and bottom strips in place; insert a corner square in each corner and join. With H hook, work 1 row of color-over-color sc around the entire joined piece, working 3 sc in each corner. With medium sea green, make 4 crocheted chains, each long enough (approximately 24 inches) to cover the two seams along the inside of each corner square; sew them in place chain side down. Block the afghan lightly.

#1 TREE OF LIFE

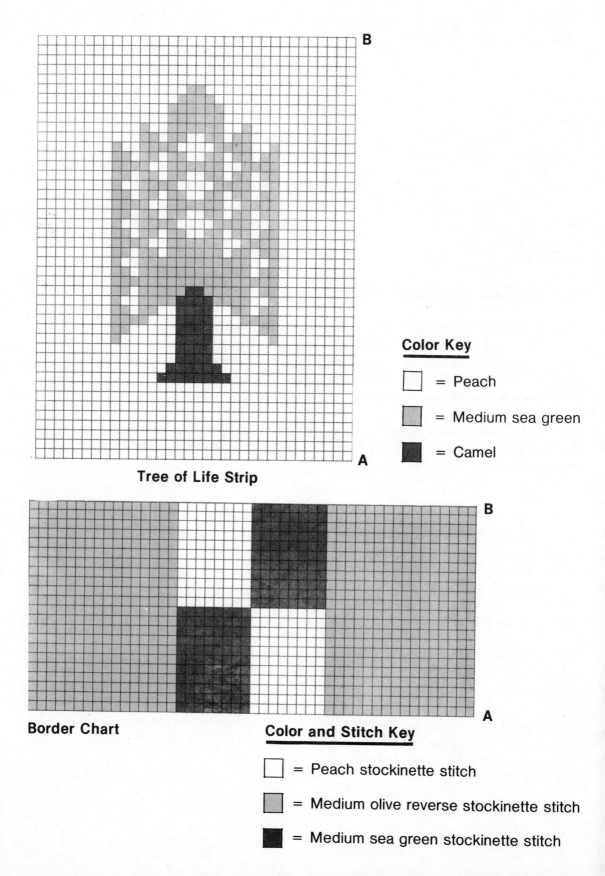

B

A

Tree of Life Strip

Color Key

☐ = Peach

▨ = Medium sea green

■ = Camel

Border Chart

B

A

Color and Stitch Key

☐ = Peach stockinette stitch

▨ = Medium olive reverse stockinette stitch

■ = Medium sea green stockinette stitch

2/ Tulips

Approximate Finished Size: 55 by 66 inches
Average Experience Needed

Diamond patches placed in the intersections of squares are traditional to the Tulip quilt, upon which this afghan is based. The usual colors for this very well-known and often photographed quilt are red, white, and green; this jazzed-up afghan version translates those colors into bright turquoise, orange, and yellow and features stylized tulips. The knitter who worked this piece reported that the colors so attracted a fellow craftswoman, she walked the length of the park to see what was being worked on.

Materials:
Columbia-Minerva Nantuk, 4-ounce balls (knitting worsted weight):
    5 balls color 5979, light jade ice (light turquoise)
    3 balls color 5705, light rust
    1 ball color 5963, yellow
    1 ball color 5734, olive
Knitting needles, No. 10½, or size required to knit to gauge
Crochet hook, size H
Yarn needle

Gauge in Stockinette Stitch: 7 stitches = 2 inches; 5 rows = 1 inch

Note: To work the stockinette st: K 1 row—right side; p 1 row—wrong side. To work the reverse stockinette st: P 1 row—right side; k 1 row—wrong side. When changing from one color and st section to another, be sure to work the first row of new color so that it appears as a k row on the right side of the work.

Center Strip: With light rust, cast on 62 sts. Referring to the chart for color and st key, work from A to B once, from C to B twice, and from C to D once. Bind off.

Side Strips: Make 1 left-side strip and 1 right-side strip. With light rust, cast on 66 sts. Referring to the chart for color and st key, work portion indicated for left- and right-side strips; rep rows of chart as for center strip. Bind off.

Patches: Make 6. With yellow, cast on 16 sts and work in stockinette st for 22 rows. Bind off.

Finishing: With yellow and H hook, work 1 row of sc around each patch, working 3 sc in each corner. Sew the three strips together. With light rust and H hook, work 1 row of sc around the entire joined piece, working 3 sc in each corner. Block lightly. Sew the yellow patches in place, diamond fashion, at the six intersections of four squares.

#2 TULIP

Color and Stitch Key

☐ = Light jade ice stockinette stitch

■ = Yellow stockinette stitch

▨ = Light rust reverse stockinette-stitch border

▨ = Light rust stockinette stitch

■ = Olive stockinette stitch

D

B

C

A

Center Strip

Left Strip

Right Strip

3 / All-White

Approximate Finished Size: 50 by 62 inches
Average Experience Needed

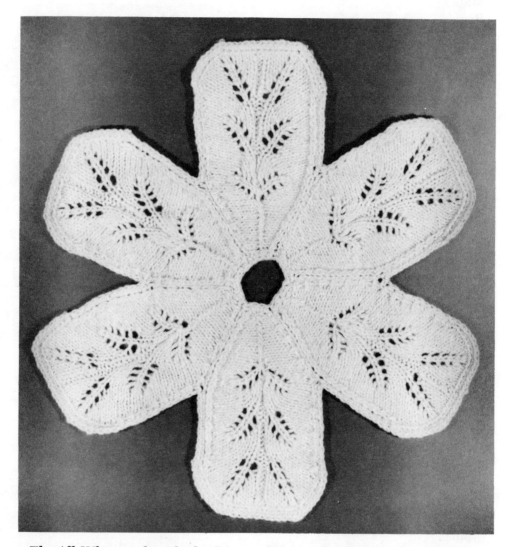

The All-White quilts relied solely on the use of elaborate topstitching for their design interest. Some of these quilts were worked with patriotic motifs, displaying eagles, state seals, and flags, often on a diamond-stitch quilted background; pineapple, fern, and feather designs were also frequently used. To create an afghan reminiscent of an All-White quilt bearing the circular fern-and-feather patterns, a slip-stitch pattern was used to create a border that has a diamond-quilted effect, and a fern-stitch pattern with yarn-overs was used to create the motif. All the work was done in a bulky natural-color wool so that the textured stitches are highlighted to their best advantage. (See p. 17 for a photograph of an All-White quilt.)

34

Materials:
Reynolds Lopi, 100-gram (3½-ounce) balls (bulky weight):
   20 balls color 51 (natural)
Knitting needles, No. 9, or size required to knit to gauge
Crochet hook, size I
Yarn Needle

Gauge in Stockinette Stitch: 3 stitches = 1 inch; 9 rows = 2 inches

Note: To work the stockinette st: K 1 row — right side; p 1 row — wrong side. Note that the center flower is made separately and appliquéd onto the background later.

Center Flower Petals: Make 6. Cast on 29 sts.
Row 1: K 1, sl 1, k 2 tog, psso, k 9, yo, k 1, yo, p 2, yo, k 1, yo, k 9, sl 1, k 2 tog, psso.
Row 2 and all other even-numbered rows: P 13, k 2, p 14.
Row 3: K 1, sl 1, k 2 tog, psso, k 8, (yo ,k 1) twice, p 2, (k 1, yo) twice, k 8, sl 1, k 2 tog, psso.
Row 5: K 1, sl 1, k 2 tog, psso, k 7, yo, k 1, yo, k 2, p 2, k 2, yo, k 1, yo, k 7, sl 1, k 2 tog, psso.
Row 7: K 1, sl 1, k 2 tog, psso, k 6, yo, k 1, yo, k 3, p 2, k 3, yo, k 1, yo, k 6, sl 1, k 2 tog, psso.
Row 9: K 1, sl 1, k 2 tog, psso, k 5, yo, k 1, yo, k 4, p 2, k 4, yo, k 1, yo, k 5, sl 1, k 2 tog, psso.
Rep Rows 1 through 9 twice more. Bind off.

Center Square: Cast on 90 sts. Work even in stockinette st for 30 inches. Bind off.
Side Borders: Make 2. Cast on 29 sts.
Rows 1, 3, 5, and 7 (wrong side): P.
Row 2: K 1, *carrying yarn in front of work, sl 3 sts as if to p, k 1, rep from * across.
Row 4: K 2, *pick up yarn and k tog with next st, k 3, rep from * across, ending pick up yarn and k tog with next st, k 2.
Row 6: K 3, *carrying yarn in front of work, sl 3 sts as if to p, k 1, rep from * across, ending k 2.
Row 8: K 4, *pick up yarn and k tog with next st, k 3, rep from * across, ending k 1.
Rep Rows 1 through 8 until piece measures 60 inches from beg. Bind off.

Top and Bottom Borders: Make 1 each. Cast on 89 sts. Work as for side border for 15 inches. Bind off.

Finishing: Sew the V-shaped, cast-on edges of each petal together, one half to another half. Sew petals of flower together as shown in the photograph. Work 1 row of sc around center hole and outer edge of flower. Work 2 rows of sc through back lps only around each of side, top, bottom, and center pieces, working 3 sc in each corner. Sew flower to center square. Join remaining pieces to center square and work 2 rows sc through back lps only around outer edge of joined afghan, working 3 sc in each corner.

4/ Joseph's Necktie

Approximate Finished Size: 50 by 65 inches
Average Experience Needed

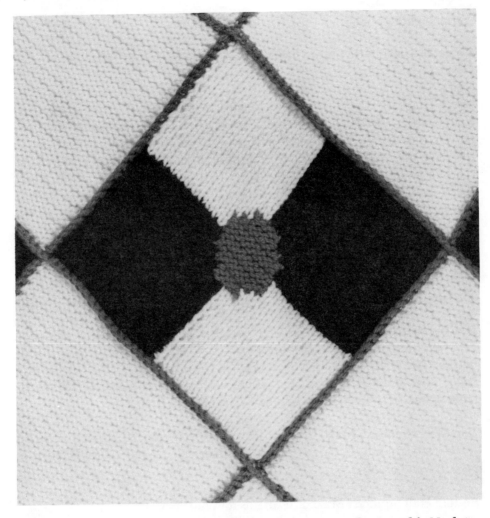

Also known as Bow Tie and Gentleman's Bow Tie, the Joseph's Necktie quilt design was usually worked with patterned fabric for the "bow tie" squares and a solid color for the contrasting squares. For this knitted afghan we chose to work with solid red, black, and off-white in order to achieve a bold geometric effect suitable for even the most contemporary decor. To give the piece added texture, the squares were joined with a single crochet stitch, which created a ridge between the squares; for added contrast, the single crochet was worked in red.

Materials:

Pingouin Pingoland, 50-gram (1¾-ounce) balls (bulky weight):
   33 balls color 853, écru (off-white)
   11 balls color 833, noir (black)
   13 balls color 831, feu (red)
Knitting needles, No. 10½, or size required to knit to gauge
Crochet hook, size K
Yarn needle

Gauge in Stockinette Stitch: 8 stitches = 3 inches; 4 rows = 1 inch

Note: To work the stockinette st: K 1 row—right side; p 1 row—wrong side. To work the reverse stockinette st: P 1 row—right side; k 1 row—wrong side. When changing from one color and st section to another, be sure to work the first row of new color so that it appears as a k row on the right side of the work. To make joining the afghan pieces easier, label the half squares and corners (left side, top, corner A, etc.) as you make them.

Necktie Squares: Make 12. With black, cast on 15 sts; then, with off-white, cast on another 15 sts. Follow chart No. 1 to completion. Bind off.

Plain Squares: Make 6. With off-white, cast on 30 sts. Work even in reverse stockinette st for 44 rows. Bind off.

Half Squares:
Left Side: Make 3. With off-white, cast on 30 sts. Work in reverse stockinette st, dec on left edge as shown on chart No. 2.
Right Side: Make 3. With off-white, cast on 1 st and work in reverse stockinette st, inc on right edge as shown on chart No. 3. Bind off.

Top Half Squares: Make 2. With off-white, cast on 30 sts and work in reverse stockinette st, dec as shown on chart No. 2 but on right edge of piece instead of left.

Bottom Half Squares: Make 2. Work as for chart No. 3.

Corners: Make 1 from each of the charts shown, working in reverse stockinette st. (chart No. 4).
Corner A: Cast on 30 sts, dec on each edge as shown on chart.
Corner B: Cast on 1 st, inc on right edge as shown on chart.
Corner C: Cast on 1 st as for corner B, working inc on left edge instead of right.
Corner D: Cast on 2 sts, inc on each edge as shown on chart.

Finishing: With red, and following diagram for placement, join squares and corner pieces into large piece by working on right side of work with sc. (Be sure that rows of reverse stockinette st on separate pieces all run in the same direction.) Work 3 rows of sc around joined piece, working 3 sc in each corner.

4 JOSEPH'S NECKTIE

Chart No. 1

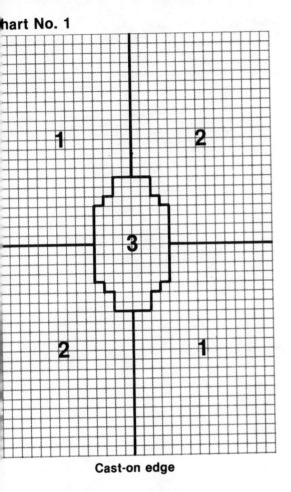

Cast-on edge

Chart No. 2

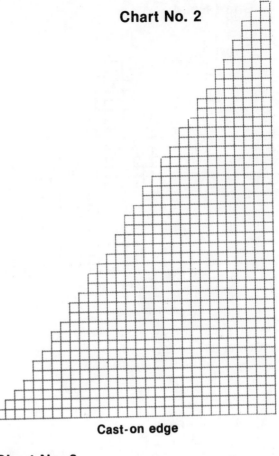

Cast-on edge

Chart No. 3

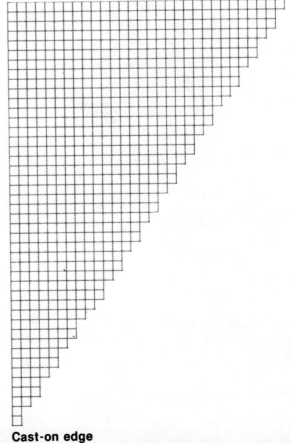

Cast-on edge

Color and Stitch Key

1 = Off-white stockinette stitch

2 = Black reverse stockinette stitch

3 = Red reverse stockinette stitch

Chart No. 4

Corner A:

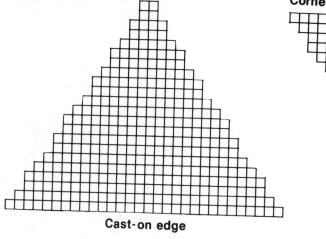

Cast-on edge

Corner D:

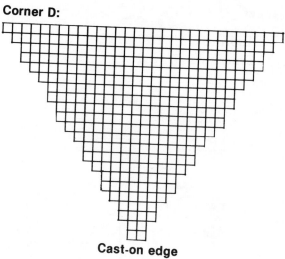

Cast-on edge

Corner B:

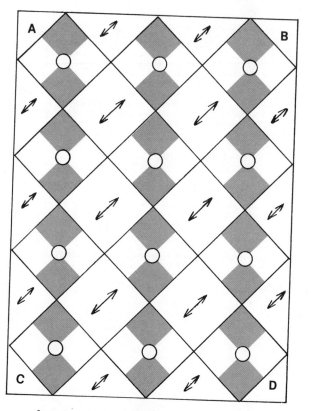

Cast-on edge

Arrows show direction of placement
of reverse stockinette rows

Corner C: Reverse corner B.

5 / Goose Tracks

Approximate Finished Size: 63 by 81 inches
Experience Needed

The familiar Goose Tracks pattern is one of many quilt designs that were based on animal tracks and bore such names as Bear's Paw, Turkey Tracks, and Crow's Foot. It was common for designs to be derived from nature and the circumstances of daily life, but this knitted afghan has been elevated to the uncommon through the use of mohair yarns in powder blue and white; the effect is soft and sophisticated. Knitted as an oversize afghan, this piece will cover a small single bed.

Materials:

Phildar Vizir, 50-gram (1¾-ounce) balls (mohair/wool/acrylic blend):
    14 balls color 43, hortensia (powder blue)
    14 balls color 10, blanc (white)
Knitting needles, No. 10½, or size required to knit to gauge
Crochet hook, size I
7 bobbins
Yarn needle

Gauge in Stockinette Stitch: 3 stitches = 1 inch; 17 rows = 4 inches

Note: To work the stockinette st: K 1 row—right side; p 1 row—wrong side. To work the reverse stockinette st: P 1 row—right side; k 1 row—wrong side. When changing from one color and st section to another, be sure to work the first row of new color so that it appears as a k row on the right side of the work. This afghan is made in three strips; use bobbins as necessary.

Center Strip: Cast on 9 sts with white, 54 sts with blue, and 9 sts with white—72 sts. Work chart to completion, rep from A to C three times, then from A to B once more. Bind off.

Side Strips: Make 2. Cast on 54 sts with blue. Work chart to completion, rep from A to C three times, then from A to B once more. Bind off.

Finishing: Sew one side strip to each long edge of center strip. Work 2 rows of color-over-color sc around outside edge of afghan, working 3 sc in each corner.

#5 GOOSE TRACKS

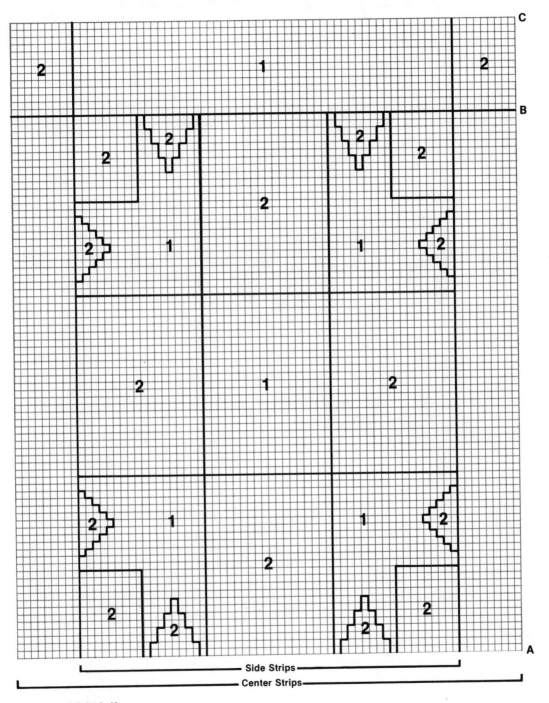

Side Strips

Center Strips

Color and Stitch Key

1 = White reverse stockinette stitch

2 = Blue stockinette stitch

6/ Flying Geese

Approximate Finished Size: 50 by 60 inches
Little Experience Needed

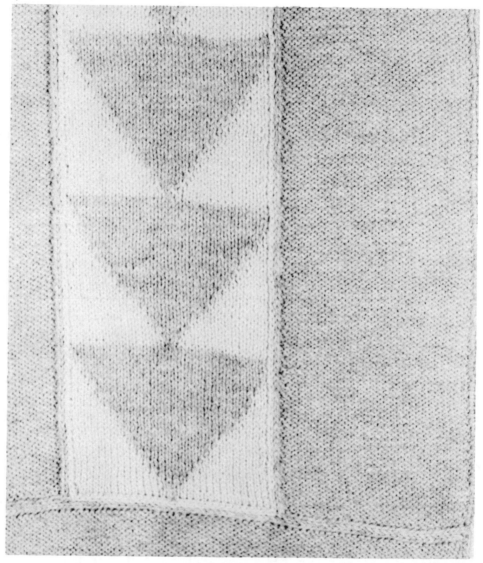

The Flying Geese of this afghan are not of the barnyard variety depicted in the previous Goose Tracks pattern but of the wild sort that seasonally migrate in formation. This design consists of a very simple triangle pattern repeat with solid-color strips set between the patterned ones and at the top and bottom. The use of beige and gray in the piece, as well as the strong geometry of its content, gives it a feeling of the art of the American Southwest.

Materials:
Phildar Pégase 206, 50-gram (1¾-ounce) balls (knitting worsted weight):
   17 balls color 35, flanelle (gray)
    6 balls color 34, fennec (gold-beige)
Knitting needles, No. 8, or size required to knit to gauge
Crochet hook, size H
Yarn needle

Gauge in Stockinette Stitch: 9 stitches = 2 inches; 6 rows = 1 inch

Note: To work the stockinette st: K 1 row — right side; p 1 row — wrong side. To work the reverse stockinette st: P 1 row — right side; k 1 row — wrong side.

Patterned Vertical Strips: Make 3. With gold-beige, cast on 29 sts. Working in stockinette st, follow 30-row chart to completion, rep it nine times in all — 270 rows. Bind off.

Solid Vertical Strips: Make 4. With gray, cast on 29 sts. Work even in reverse stockinette st for 270 rows. Bind off.

Top and Bottom Strips: Make 1 each. With gray, cast on 217 sts and work even for 6 inches. Bind off.

Finishing: With H hook and gray, work 1 row of sc around each of the solid vertical strips and the top and bottom strips, working 3 sc in each corner. With gold-beige, work 1 row of sc around each patterned vertical strip in the same manner. Join the patterned strips with the solid-color vertical strips so that a solid strip is on each outer edge and the remaining solid strips alternate with the patterned strips between. Sew the top and bottom strips in place. With H hook and gray, work 1 row of sc around entire joined piece, working 3 sc in each corner. Block piece lightly.

#6 FLYING GEESE

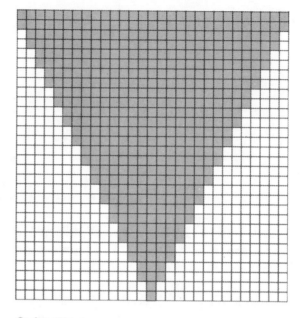

Color Key

☐ = Fennec (gold-beige)

■ = Flanelle (gray)

7 / Log Cabin

Approximate Finished Size: 48 by 48 inches
Little Experience Needed

The Log Cabin is one of the best-known of all quilt patterns. Depending on the colors used and the way in which those colors are arranged, completely different designs can be formed, some of which have been given their own names, such as Barn Raising. This Log Cabin afghan is knitted in a simple garter stitch throughout, in lovely shades of pinks and greens. If you wish to make a larger afghan, increase the number of patterned squares and border squares accordingly. (See p. 10 for a photograph of a Log Cabin quilt.)

Materials:

Dawn Wintuk 100% Du Pont Orlon acrylic, 3½-ounce skeins (knitting worsted weight):

   3 skeins color 355, spruce (dark green)
   2 skeins color 357, light jade (medium green)
   1 skein color 350, baby green (light green)
   4 skeins color 323, candy pink (light pink)
   4 skeins color 360, conch shell (dark pink)

Knitting needles, No. 9, or size required to knit to gauge
Yarn needle

Gauge in Garter Stitch: 15 stitches = 4 inches; 15 rows = 2 inches

Note: Work in garter st throughout. To work the garter st: K every row. When changing colors within a row, always twist yarn on wrong side of work to avoid leaving a gap.

Log Cabin Squares: Make 16. With spruce, cast on 30 sts. Follow chart to completion, changing colors as indicated. Bind off.

Side Squares: Make 16. With candy pink, cast on 30 sts. Work even for 30 rows. Change to conch shell. Work even for 30 rows. Bind off.

Corner Squares: Make 4. With spruce, cast on 30 sts. Work even for 60 rows. Bind off.

Finishing: Arrange log cabin squares in four groups of four squares each so that the candy-pink edges are to the inside and the spruce to the outside. Sew in place and then sew the four groups together. Sew four side squares along each side of the joined piece, with the candy-pink edges to the outside. Sew one corner square in each corner.

#7 LOG CABIN

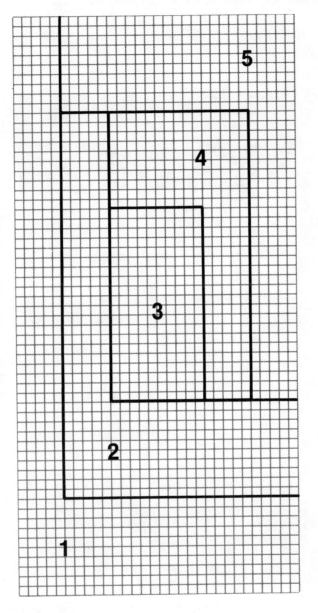

Color Key

1 = Spruce

2 = Light jade

3 = Baby green

4 = Candy pink

5 = Conch shell

8/ Homestead

Approximate Finished Size: 42 by 56 inches
No Experience Needed

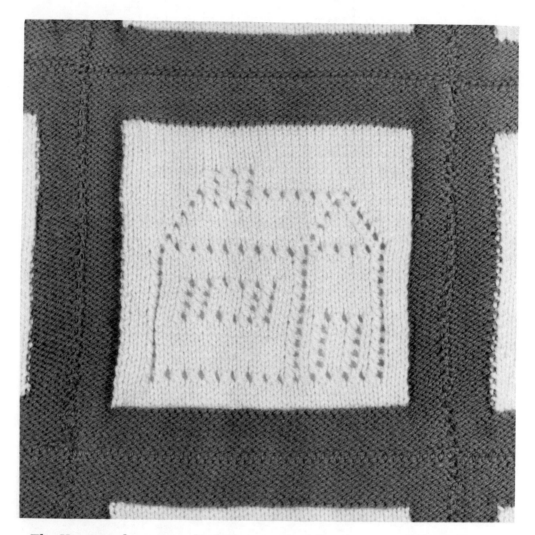

The Homestead pattern, also known as the Schoolhouse, can be seen in some of the earliest and most primitive of American quilts. One of the oldest examples of this type of quilt shows each house appliquéd in a different-patterned material with the windows and doors cut from yet another fabric. The effect is quite hodgepodge—one can imagine the worn-out dresses, aprons, bonnets, and shirts that must have been used to piece such a quilt. The knitted afghan shown here has been simplified through the use of only two colors. To define the houses and add texture, yarn-over stitches have been incorporated as outline stitches.

Materials:
Phildar Kadischa, 50-gram (1¾-ounce) balls (bulky weight):
  14 balls color 33, églantine (pink)
  14 balls color 25, cosmos (blue)
Knitting needles, No. 10½, or size required to knit to gauge
Crochet hook, size I
Yarn needle

Gauge in Stockinette Stitch: 7 stitches = 2 inches; 5 rows = 1 inch

Note: To work the stockinette st: K 1 row—right side; p 1 row—wrong side. To work the reverse stockinette st: P 1 row—right side; k 1 row—wrong side. When changing from one color and st section to another, be sure to work the first row of new color so that it appears as a k row on the right side of the work.

Squares: Make 12. With blue, cast on 48 sts. Work the 68-row chart to completion. Bind off.

Finishing: Sew the squares together in a three-square-wide by four-square-long arrangement. With blue and I hook, work 2 rows of sc around the joined piece, working 3 sc in each corner.

#8 HOMESTEAD

Row 61

Color and Stitch Key

O = Yarn over

X = Slip 1, knit 1, pass slip stitch over

☐ = Eglantine stockinette stitch

▨ = Cosmos reverse stockinette stitch

9/ Shoofly

Approximate Finished Size: 60 by 57 inches
Little Experience Needed

Because Shoofly is such a basic pattern, it has been given many other names, ranging from Chinese Coin and Grandmother's Choice to Star-Spangled Banner, depending on what it brought to mind to its maker. With the placing of the colors in a slightly different arrangement, Ohio Star, Lucky Star, and Tippecanoe and Tyler Too came into being. A few more variations and we jump into the barnyard with Corns and Beans, Hen and Chickens, and Duck and Ducklings. This Shoofly afghan, which is knitted with lightweight yarns in blue-green, beige tweed, and a deep purple, is framed with a wide striped border.

Materials:

Reynolds Town and Country, 50-gram (1¾-ounce) balls (sport weight):
  6 balls color 274 (beige tweed)
  4 balls color 203 (purple)
  3 balls color 271 (blue-green)
Knitting needles, No. 8, or size required to knit to gauge
Crochet hook, size G
Yarn needle

Gauge in Stockinette Stitch: 9 stitches = 2 inches; 6 rows = 1 inch

Note: To work the stockinette st: K 1 row — right side: p 1 row — wrong side.

Left-Side Strip: With beige tweed, cast on 90 sts. Work even in stockinette st for 20 rows. Change to blue-green on first 75 sts and, maintaining 15 sts at left edge in tweed, work for 20 rows. Change to tweed on first 60 sts and, maintaining next 15 sts in blue-green and last 15 sts in tweed, work even for 20 rows. Change to purple on first 45 sts and, maintaining next 15 sts in tweed, next 15 sts in blue-green, and last 15 sts in tweed, work even for 220 rows. Change to tweed on first 45 sts and, maintaining 15 sts each in tweed, blue-green, and tweed, work for 20 rows. Change to blue-green on first 60 sts and, maintaining next 15 sts in blue-green and last 15 sts in tweed, work even for 20 rows. Change to tweed across all sts and work even for 20 rows. Bind off.

Right-Side Strip: Work as for left-side strip, reversing order of colors so that the right angles formed by the color stripes appear at the right side of the strip instead of the left. (You are forming a frame for the center strip.)

Center Strip: With tweed, cast on 90 sts and work even in the following stripes: 20 rows tweed, 20 rows blue-green, 20 rows tweed, 50 rows purple. Now work Shoofly chart to completion, working from A to B once; then reverse the reading of the chart (simply turn the chart upside down) and work from B to C — 120 rows in all. Now work across all 90 sts in the following stripes: 50 rows purple, 20 rows tweed, 20 rows blue-green, 20 rows tweed. Bind off.

Finishing: Sew strips together, carefully matching stripes. With G hook and tweed, work 1 row of sc around entire joined piece, working 3 sc in each corner. Block piece lightly.

#9 SHOOFLY

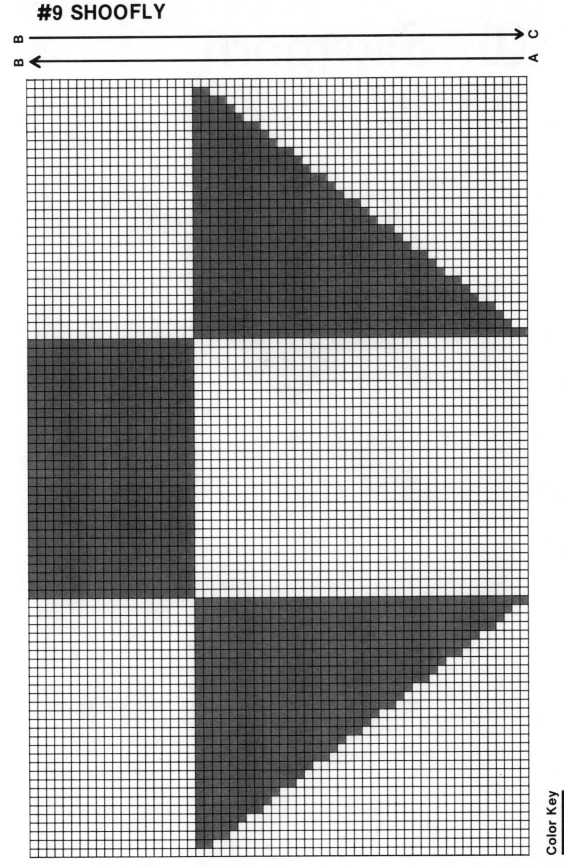

B B → C

B ← A

Color Key

□ = Beige tweed ■ = Blue-green

10 / Sawtooth

Approximate Finished Size: 43 by 54 inches
Average Experience Needed

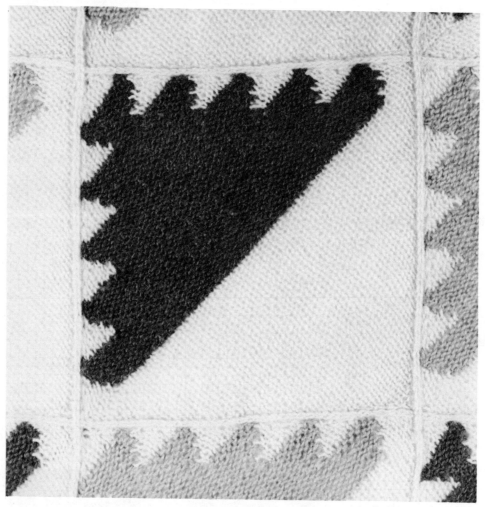

The name Sawtooth for this design is self-explanatory. The pattern is one of the oldest known and was most often worked in varicolored prints against a solid-color background. Our knitted translation is delightfully light and soft, and the solid colors used — navy, powder blue, and peach — emphasize the strong geometry of the design. A delicate, scalloped border worked around the outside edge softens the hard-edge quality of the motif.

Materials:
Reynolds Kitten, 50-gram (1¾-ounce) balls (fluffy sport weight):
   6 balls color 70 (peach)
   2 balls color 12 (navy blue)
   2 balls color 15 (powder blue)
Knitting needles, No. 8, or size required to knit to gauge
Crochet hook, size G
Yarn needle

Gauge in Stockinette Stitch: 13 stitches = 4 inches; 6 rows = 1 inch

Note: To work the stockinette st: K 1 row—right side; p 1 row—wrong side. When changing from one color and st section to another, be sure to work the first row of new color so that it appears as a k row on the right side of the work.

Squares: Make 10 in peach/navy blue combination; 10 in peach/powder blue combination. With peach, cast on 3 sts. Work in stockinette st, inc 1 st each edge every other row, as indicated on chart. Work color and stitch changes and decs as indicated on chart. Bind off remaining 3 sts.

Finishing: Sew squares together in a four-square-wide by five-square-long arrangement, alternating peach/navy blue and peach/powder blue squares within each horizontal and vertical row. With peach and G hook, crochet three chains, each long enough to cover one of the three vertical seams, and four chains, each long enough to cover one of the four horizontal seams; sew in place.

Edging:
Rnd 1: With peach, work 1 row of sc around entire joined piece, with 3 sc in each corner; join with sl st to first st.
Rnd 2: *Work 3 sc in next sc and 1 sl st in next sc; rep from * around. Fasten off.

#10 SAWTOOTH

Color and Stitch Key

☐ = Peach stockinette stitch

■ = Navy or powder blue reverse stockinette stitch

2

Knitted Lap Robes

11/ Roman Stripe

Approximate Finished Size: 42 by 56 inches
No Experience Needed

The Roman Stripe pattern, though one of the simplest, can have a very striking, modern effect, depending on the colors chosen. The pattern is also known as Roman Square and, when the stripe of each square is alternated, vertically and horizontally, as it has been here, as the Roman Stripe Zigzag. Because this knitted translation of the Roman Stripe is worked in simple garter stitch throughout, it is the perfect beginner's project; use the soft light jade, apricot, and baby-blue color combination we chose, or work out your own color scheme.

Materials:
Dawn Wintuk 100% Du Pont Orlon acrylic 3½-ounce skeins (knitting worsted weight):
    4 skeins color 357, light jade
    4 skeins color 310, apricot
    4 skeins color 312, baby blue
Knitting needles, No. 9, or size required to knit to gauge
Yarn needle

Gauge in Garter Stitch: 7 stitches = 2 inches; 7 rows = 1 inch

Note: Work in garter st throughout. To work the garter st: K every row.

Squares: Make 10 in apricot/baby blue combination; 10 in light jade/baby blue combination. With apricot or light jade, cast on 40 sts and work even in garter st for 26 rows. Change to baby blue and work even for 26 rows. Change back to first color (apricot or light jade) and work even for 26 rows. Bind off.

Finishing: Sew squares together in a four-square-wide by five-square-long arrangement, alternating the color of the squares and the direction in which the garter-st rows run — place the jade/blue squares so that the rows run vertically and the apricot/blue squares so that the rows run horizontally.

12 / Baskets

Approximate Finished Size: 38 by 42 inches
Average Experience Needed

*There are many, many varieties of Basket quilts, most of them
depicting, and named for, anything that can be put into a
basket—Flower Basket, Garden Basket, Basket of Oranges, Cherry
Basket. Since today wicker baskets, on which these designs were based,
have been relegated to purely decorative use, it is only the popularity of
the basket in nineteenth-century quilt designs that reminds us of how
much a part of daily life it was—among other things, it was used for
gathering fruit and vegetables, flowers, herbs, and eggs. The promise of
an empty basket waiting to be filled with something pretty and/or
delicious is here in our knitted lap robe that features cabled borders and
patch corners. (See p. 12 for a photograph of a Basket quilt.)*

Materials:
Coats & Clark Red Heart 4-ply hand-knitting yarn, 99.2-gram (3½-ounce) skeins (knitting worsted weight):
  6 skeins color 3, off-white
  2 skeins color 588, amethyst
Knitting needles, No. 9, or size required to knit to gauge
Cable-stitch holder
Crochet hook, size H
Yarn needle

Gauge in Stockinette Stitch: 4 stitches = 1 inch; 5 rows = 1 inch

Note: To work the stockinette st: K 1 row — right side; p 1 row — wrong side. To work the reverse stockinette st: P 1 row — right side; k 1 row — wrong side.

Basket Strips: Make 2. With off-white, cast on 56 sts. Work even in stockinette st, following chart for color changes; work from A to B once and then from C to B once. Bind off.

Corner Squares: Make 4. With amethyst, cast on 22 sts. Work even in reverse stockinette st for 30 rows. Bind off.

Border Side Strips: Make 2. With off-white, cast on 27 sts.
Row 1: *K 1, p 4, sl next 2 sts onto holder, hold in back of work, k next 2 sts, k 2 sts from holder, p 4, rep from * once more, and end k 1.
Row 2 and all other even-numbered rows: Work sts as they appear (purl the p sts; knit the k sts).
Row 3: *K 1, p 3, (sl next p st onto holder, hold in back of work, k next 2 sts, p st from holder — right twist — RT — made), (sl 2 sts onto holder, hold in front of work, p next st, k 2 sts from holder — left twist — LT — made), p 3, rep from * once more, and end k 1.
Row 5: *K 1, p 2, RT, p 2, LT, p 2, rep from * once more, and end k 1.
Row 7: *K 1, p 1, RT, p 4, LT, p 1, rep from * once more, and end k 1.
Row 9: *K 1, RT, p 6, LT, rep from * once more, and end k 1.
Row 11: *K 1, LT, p 6, RT, rep from * once more, and end k 1.
Row 13: *K 1, p 1, LT, p 4, RT, p 1, rep from * once more, and end k 1.
Row 15: *K 1, p 2, LT, p 2, RT, p 2, rep from * once more, and end k 1.
Row 17: *K 1, p 3, LT, RT, p 3, rep from * once more, and end k 1.
Row 18: Work all sts as they appear.
Rep Row 1 through 18 eleven times more. Bind off.

Top and Bottom Border Strips: Make 1 each. Work as for the side strips, rep Rows 1 through 18 nine times. Bind off.

Finishing: Sew basket strips together. Pin border strips in place, easing in any fullness, and join to basket strips. Sew one corner square in each corner. With H hook, work 1 row of color-over-color sc around entire joined piece, working 3 sc in each corner. With amethyst, work a second row of sc around the piece, working through the back lps only of previous row and working 3 sc in each corner. With amethyst, crochet a chain long enough to fit around the inner edge of the border; sew in place, chain side down. Block piece lightly.

#12 BASKETS

B

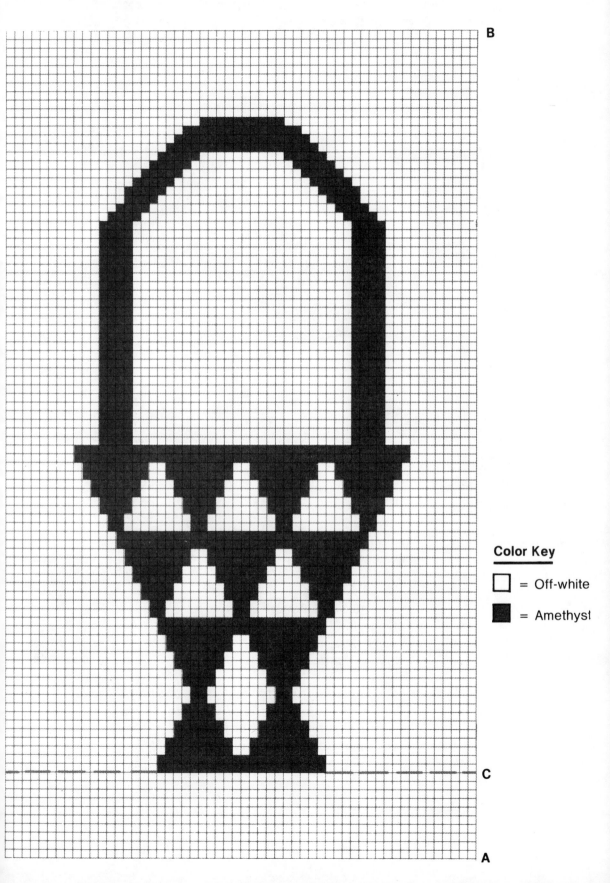

C

A

Color Key

☐ = Off-white

■ = Amethyst

13 / Indian Hatchet

Approximate Finished Size: 38 by 47 inches
No Experience Needed

Indian Hatchet takes its name from the light-colored center diagonal
stripe of each square. One of the simplest of all quilts, it was often the
project on which a little girl might sew her first stitches. To make our
knitted lap robe, the squares are worked on the diagonal in a simple
garter stitch.

Materials:
Dawn Sayelle, 3½-ounce skeins (knitting worsted weight):
  2 skeins color 328, turquoise
  2 skeins color 335, purple
  2 skeins color 321, lavender
  2 skeins color 356, forest green
Knitting needles, No. 9, or size required to knit to gauge
Yarn needle

Gauge in Garter Stitch: 4 stitches = 1 inch; 15 rows = 2 inches

Note: Work in garter st throughout. To work the garter st: K every row. Incs and decs are worked on every other row throughout.

Squares: Make 10 squares in forest green/turquoise combination; 10 squares in purple/lavender combination. With forest green or purple, cast on 3 sts. Work even for 2 rows. On next and every other row, inc 1 st each edge until there are 35 sts. Work 1 row even. On next row, change to turquoise or lavender and continue to inc until there are 53 sts. Work 1 row even. On next and every other row, dec 1 st each edge until there are 37 sts. Work 1 row even. On next row, change to forest green or purple and continue to dec until there are 3 sts left. Bind off remaining 3 sts.

Finishing: Alternating the colors of the squares and placing them so that the light-colored "hatchets" run on the diagonal (see photo), sew the squares together in a four-square-wide by five-square-long arrangement.

14/ Double Irish Chain

Approximate Finished Size: 37 by 49 inches
Average Experience Needed

This lap robe draws upon the Double Irish Chain pattern, though there are also Single Irish Chain and Triple Irish Chain quilts, some of which have a flower or shamrock appliquéd in the center of each diamond shape. Quilts appliquéd with shamrocks are called Double Irish Cross; this pattern is often quilted in squares the size of those in the chain. The knitted lap robe shown here uses a solid Double Irish Chain as a border (the word "double" refers to the use of two colors) and, for texture, a simple basket weave stitch, which also recalls the plain Double Irish Cross.

Materials:

Reynolds Highland Worsted, 100-gram (3½-ounce) balls (knitting worsted weight):

   4 balls color 454, peach
   1 ball color 422, fern green
   1 ball color 490, rust

Knitting needles, No. 9, or size required to knit to gauge
Yarn needle

Gauge in Stockinette Stitch: 9 stitches = 2 inches; 16 rows = 3 inches

Note: To work the stockinette st: K 1 row — right side; p 1 row — wrong side. To work the reverse stockinette st: P 1 row — right side; k 1 row — wrong side. When changing from one color and st section to another, be sure to work the first row of new color so that it appears as a k row on the right side of the work.

Strips: With peach, cast on 54 sts. Referring to chart for color and st changes, make 1 each of strips A, B, and C.

Finishing: Sew strips together. Block piece lightly.

#14 DOUBLE IRISH CHAIN

Strip A   Strip B   Strip C

Color and Stitch Key

O   = 6 sts / 8 rows in peach stockinette stitch

X   = 6 sts / 8 rows in peach reverse stockinette stitch

■ (light)   = 6 sts / 8 rows in rust stockinette stitch

■ (dark)   = 6 sts / 8 rows in fern green stockinette

3

Knitted
Baby Blankets

15 / Cats and Mice

Approximate Finished Size: 28 by 37 inches

Average Experience Needed

It is difficult to figure out the way in which Cats and Mice got its name; the fact that the design is also known as Beggar's Block doesn't help. In any case, this strong, geometric pattern can be surprisingly soft in appearance when pastels are used, as has been done here with the baby colors of blue, pink, and off-white.

Materials:

Lane Borgosesia Stagioni, 100-gram (3½-ounce) balls (knitting worsted weight):

   2 balls color 2428 (off-white)
   2 balls color 1912 (pink)
   2 balls color 410 (blue)

Knitting needles, No. 8, or size required to knit to gauge
Crochet hook, size H
Yarn needle

Gauge in Stockinette Stitch: 4 stitches = 1 inch; 6 rows = 1 inch

Note: To work the stockinette st: K 1 row — right side; p 1 row — wrong side. To work the reverse stockinette st: P 1 row — right side; k 1 row — wrong side.

Square A: Make 4. With off-white, cast on 36 sts. Work even in stockinette st, following chart A to completion. Bind off.

Square B: Make 4. With pink, cast on 36 sts. Work even in stockinette st, following chart B to completion. Bind off.

Center Square: With off-white, cast on 36 sts. Work even for 48 rows in reverse stockinette st. Bind off.

Top and Bottom Border Strips: Make 1 each. With blue, cast on 114 sts. Work even in reverse stockinette st for 6 inches. Bind off.

Finishing: With H hook, work 1 row of color-over-color sc around each square and each of the top and bottom border strips, working 3 sc in each corner. Sew the squares together, positioning the center square in the middle, one of the square-A pieces in each corner, and one square-B piece on each side. Sew the border strips to the top and bottom of the joined piece. Work 1 row of blue sc around the entire joined piece, working 3 sc in each corner.

#15 CATS AND MICE

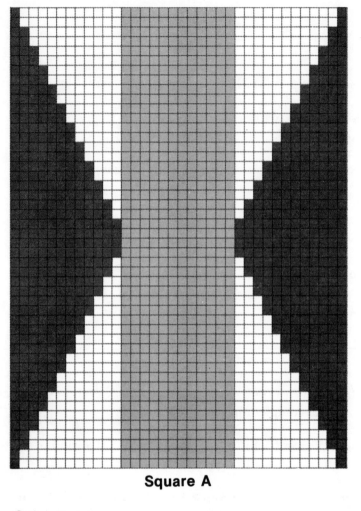

Square A

Color Key

☐ = Off-white

■ = Pink

▨ = Blue

Square B

16/ Baby Blocks

Approximate Finished Size: 30 by 40 inches
Experience Needed

The Baby Blocks, or Diamond, quilt pattern utilizes three shades ranging from light to dark to create the optical illusion of three-dimensional cubes. Even though this is a very modern-looking design, it is the basis for many nineteenth-century quilts. One of the most famous Diamond quilts was made from the red, white, and blue bunting that decorated a podium in Illinois from which President Lincoln once spoke. The knitted Baby Blocks crib blanket shown here is worked in shades of pink, lavender, and dark purple to create a strong cubic effect. (See p. 8 for a photograph of a Baby Blocks quilt.)

Materials:
Pingouin Pingochamp, 100-gram (3½-ounce) skeins (knitting worsted weight):
    4 skeins color 363, lupin (lavender)
    4 skeins color 314, pink
    4 skeins color 310, aubergine (purple)
Knitting needles, No. 9, or size required to knit to gauge
Crochet hook, size G
Yarn needle

Gauge in Stockinette Stitch: 4 stitches = 1 inch; 11 rows = 2 inches

Note: To work the stockinette st: K 1 row—right side; p 1 row—wrong side. To work the reverse stockinette st: P 1 row—right side; k 1 row—wrong side. When changing from one color and st section to another, be sure to work the first row of new color so that it appears as a k row on the right side of the work. The center portion of this afghan, including the top and bottom borders, is worked in one piece; the side borders and corners are worked separately.

Bottom Border for Center Portion: With lavender, cast on 71 sts. Work even in reverse stockinette st for 10 rows. Then work 10 rows pink and 10 rows purple.

Center Baby-Block Section: Change to stockinette st and follow the chart to completion.

Top Border for Center Portion: Change to reverse stockinette st and work 10 rows purple, 10 rows pink, and 10 rows lavender. Bind off.

Side Borders: Make 2. With purple, cast on 112 sts and work even in reverse stockinette st for 10 rows. Then work 10 rows pink and 10 rows lavender. Bind off.

Corners: Make 4. With purple, cast on 22 sts and work even in reverse stockinette st for 30 rows. Bind off.

Finishing: Sew side borders and corner pieces in place. With G hook, work 1 row of color-over-color sc around entire joined piece, working 3 sc in each corner. With purple, work 1 row of sc around entire joined piece in same manner.

#16 BABY BLOCKS

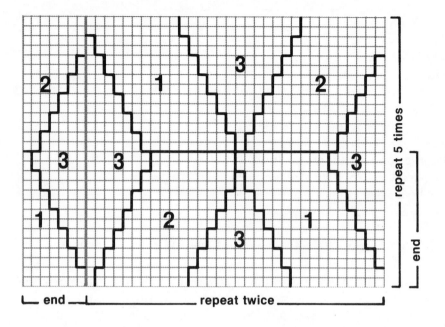

Color Key

1 = Lavender

2 = Purple

3 = Pink

17 / Interlocking Squares

Approximate Finished Size: 30 by 38 inches
No Experience Needed

The Interlocking Squares pattern is not a common quilt design, but it was chosen to be included here as one that could be adapted to a piece that a beginner could knit. Only two stitches are used — the double seed stitch and the garter stitch. The only portion of the work that requires some special care is the piecing together of the sides of the squares when they are appliquéd to the background piece.

79

Materials:
Columbia-Minerva Nantuk, 4-ounce balls (knitting worsted weight):
  2 balls color 5704, peach
  2 balls color 5965, medium sea green
  1 ball color 5733, medium olive
Knitting needles, No. 10, or size required to knit to gauge
Crochet hook, size H
Yarn needle

Gauge in Pattern Stitch: 4 stitches = 1 inch; 6 rows = 1 inch

Note: To work the garter st: K every row. The base of this blanket is worked in one piece; the interlocking squares are worked separately and sewn on later.

Pattern Stitch (Double Seed Stitch):
Row 1 (right side): *K 2, p 2, rep from * across.
Row 2: *K 2, p 2, rep from * across.
Row 3: *P 2, k 2, rep from * across.
Row 4: *P 2, k 2, rep from * across.

Blanket: With medium sea green, cast on 120 sts. Work even in garter st for 36 rows. Change to peach and pat st and work even for 30 inches, ending with a wrong-side row. Change to sea green and garter st and work even for 36 rows. Bind off.

Square Side Pieces: Make 4 in sea green, 4 in medium olive. Cast on 60 sts. Work even in garter st for 14 rows. Bind off.

Finishing: With peach and H hook, work 1 row of sc along each side edge of pat-st section. Sew side pieces in place, using photo as guide. (Notice that the side pieces cut into each other at the corners; that is, there is only a partial joining at the points where the short edges of the strips meet.)

Clockwise from top: *Interlocking Squares*, p.79; *Roman Stripe*, p.60; *Tree of Life*, p.28

Bottom to top: *Indian Hatchet, p.66; Baskets, p.62; Baby Blocks, p.76*

Clockwise from left: *North Carolina Lily, p.115; Log Cabin, p.47; Homestead, p.50*

Clockwise from top: *Dresden Plates, p.106; Bridal Wreath, p.96; Joseph's Necktie, p.37*

Clockwise from left: *Grandmother's Fan, p.109; Tulips, p.31; Baby's Flower Garden, p.141; All-White, p.34*

Double Irish Chain, p.68

Clockwise from top: *Trip Around the World, p.138; Zigzag, p.124; Yo-yo, p.132*

Shoofly, p.53

18 / Baby's Nine-Patch

Approximate Finished Size: 31 by 41 inches
Average Experience Needed

Nine-patch squares are the basis for many of the earliest of quilts. The squares can be joined vertically and horizontally, as they are in this Baby's Nine-Patch; they can be turned diagonally; or they can be worked as corner patches into a number of other designs. As a quilting design, it makes good use of fabric scraps; as an afghan, it is an equally good way to use up yarn scraps. If you wish to use your own color scheme, plan out your design in advance with crayons or felt-tipped markers.

Materials:

Lane Borgosesia Stagioni, 100-gram (3½-ounce) balls (knitting worsted weight):

   6 balls color 2428 (off-white)
   3 balls color 1912 (pink)
   3 balls color 410 (blue)
   5 balls color 1940 (purple)

Knitting needles, No. 8, or size required to knit to gauge

Crochet hook, size H

Yarn needle

Gauge in Stockinette Stitch: 4 stitches = 1 inch; 6 rows = 1 inch

Note: MC = main color (off-white); CC = contrast color (pink, purple, or blue). To work the stockinette st: K 1 row—right side; p 1 row—wrong side. To work the reverse stockinette st: P 1 row—right side; k 1 row—wrong side. When changing from one color and st section to another, be sure to work the first row of new color so that it appears as a k row on the right side of the work.

Patchwork Squares: Make 3 in pink/off-white combination; 3 in blue/off-white combination; 6 in purple/off-white combination. Cast on 12 sts with CC, 12 sts MC, 12 sts in same CC—36 sts. Follow 46-row chart to completion. Bind off.

Horizontal Strips: Make 9. With MC, cast on 36 sts. Work even in reverse stockinette st for 10 rows. Bind off.

Vertical Strips: Make 8. With MC, cast on 8 sts. Work even in reverse stockinette st for 46 rows. Bind off.

Small Patches: Make 2 with each CC (6 altogether). Cast on 8 sts. Work even in reverse stockinette st for 10 rows. Bind off.

Finishing: With H hook, work 1 row of sc in matching CC around each patchwork square and small patch, working 3 sc in each corner. In same manner, work 1 row of sc with MC around three of the nine horizontal strips. Edge three of the remaining six horizontal strips as follows: With MC, sc around the two long edges and the right short edge; edge each left short edge with a different CC. Edge the remaining three horizontal strips on the two long edges and left short edge with MC; edge each right short edge with a different CC. Edge four of the eight vertical strips with MC only. Edge the remaining four vertical strips on three sides with MC, edging the top short edge of two of them with pink sc and the bottom short edge of the remaining two with blue. Join the pieces of the afghan together as shown in the placement diagram.

#18 BABY'S NINE-PATCH

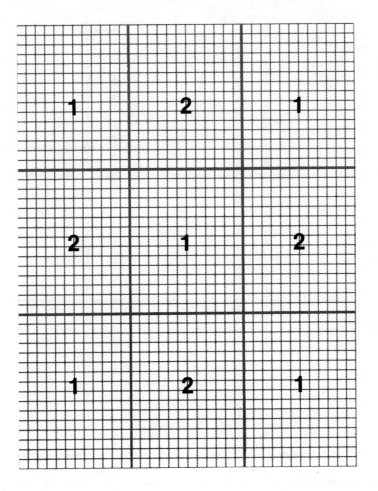

Color and Stitch Key

1 = Reverse stockinette stitch
    in CC

2 = Stockinette stitch in MC

#18 BABY'S NINE-PATCH

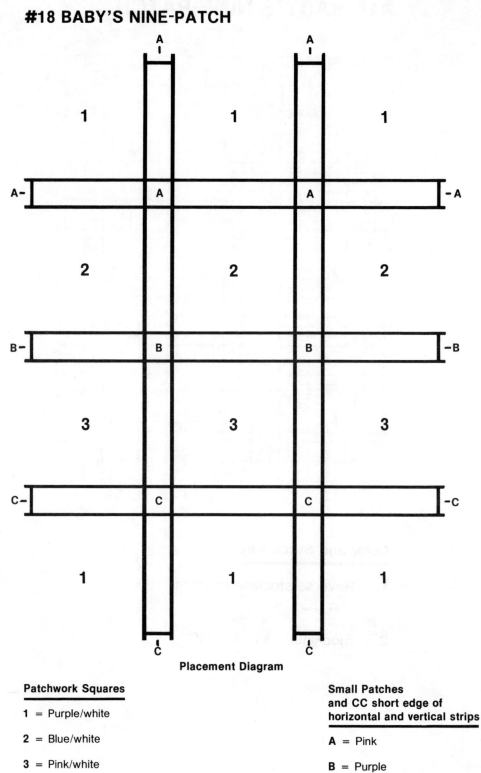

Placement Diagram

Patchwork Squares

1 = Purple/white

2 = Blue/white

3 = Pink/white

**Small Patches
and CC short edge of
horizontal and vertical strips**

A = Pink

B = Purple

C = Blue

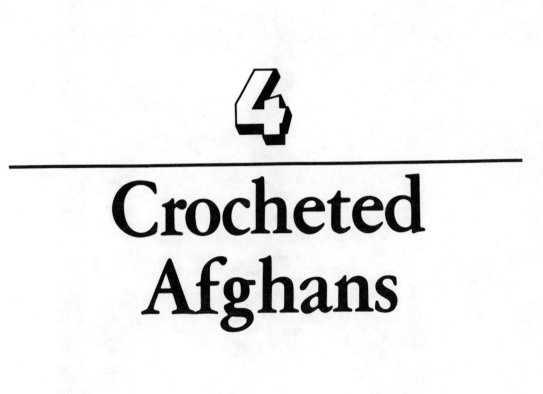

4

Crocheted Afghans

19/ Wedding Ring

Approximate Finished Size: 54 by 58 inches
Average Experience Needed

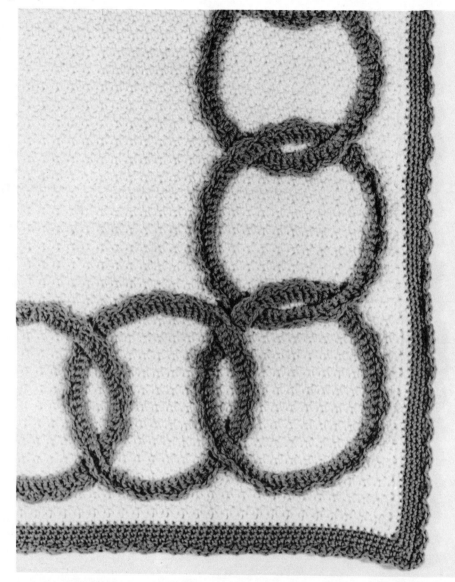

Both Wedding Ring and Double Wedding Ring quilts were made in two ways. The curved type displays appliquéd rings that overlap, each ring of which is often comprised of varicolored patches. The more geometric type is made of blocks with color sections separated diagonally, so that the rings appear more octagonal than round and do not overlap. The first type is far more common. For the crocheted afghan shown here, overlapping solid-color wedding rings have been appliquéd around the border only. If you wish, you can go on from there and cover the entire background surface with overlapping rings. (See p. 16 for a photograph of a Double Wedding Ring quilt.)

Materials:
Pingouin Le Yarn 2, 100-gram (3½-ounce) skeins (knitting worsted weight):
    11 skeins color 03, natural
     4 skeins color 45, medium blue
Crochet hook, size I, or size required to crochet to gauge
Yarn needle

Gauge in Pattern Stitch: 3 stitches = 1 inch

Strips: Make 3. With natural, ch 54 loosely.
Row 1: Work 1 sc in second ch from hook, *1 dc in next ch, 1 sc in next ch, rep from * across. Ch 2 and turn.
Row 2: Work 1 dc in each sc and 1 sc in each dc. Ch 1 to turn if the row ends with 1 dc; ch 2 to turn if row ends with 1 sc. Rep Row 2 for pat.
Work even for 56 inches. Fasten off.

Wedding Rings: Make 26. With blue, ch 72 and join with sl st to form a ring.
Rnd 1: Ch 2 (counts as 1 dc), work 1 dc in each ch around except work 2 dc in each eighteenth ch — 76 dc.
Rnd 2: Work *1 sl st in next dc, skip 1 dc, 3 dc in next dc, skip 1 dc, rep from * around, join with sl st to first st. Fasten off.
Work the remaining rings in the same way but insert 72-st chain through the center of previous ring before joining the chain with sl st, being careful not to twist it.

Finishing: Sew strips together. With natural, work 1 row of sc around entire joined piece, working 3 sc in each corner. With blue, work 4 rnds of sc around in same manner.

Scalloped Edging: Continuing with blue, *work 3 dc in next st, skip next st, 1 sl st in next st, skip next st, rep from * around, join with sl st to first st. Fasten off. Leaving a 2-inch border all around, pin wedding rings in place on the afghan, placing one ring in each corner with six rings between the corner rings on the long sides and five between on the short sides. (A plate 8 inches in diameter is useful as a guide for pinning perfect circles.) Sew the rings in place and block the piece lightly.

20 / Mosaic

Approximate Finished Size: 47 by 58 inches
Experience Needed

Mosaic quilts, based on a hexagon-shaped module, are limitless in their variety and, consequently, their names. Flower Garden, French Bouquet, Honeycomb, Job's Trouble, and Spider Web are just a few of the names for the motif arrangement that can be seen at the center of this rust, peach, and royal blue crocheted afghan. The making of each hexagon is very simple, but some care must be taken when joining the hexagons into the various components of the afghan. Though the piece is time-consuming, it is perfect "carry-along" work and will certainly be treasured by its owner for years to come. (See p. 9 for a photograph of a Mosaic quilt.)

Materials:
Lane Borgosesia Knitaly, 100-gram (3½-ounce) skeins (knitting worsted weight):
   9 skeins color 1252 (peach)
   7 skeins color 169 (rust)
   4 skeins color 1415 (blue)
Crochet hook, size H, or size required to crochet to gauge
Yarn needle

Gauge: Each hexagon = 2½ inches in diameter

Note: The "wrong sides" of the hexagons are used as the right side of the work in this afghan, and they are referred to as such in the following instructions. In this project, the hexagons have been joined in five different ways to make five different components to facilitate the joining of the afghan. Refer to the charts to determine how many hexagons and of what colors are required for each component.

Basic Hexagon (first hexagon of any component): Ch 4 and join with sl st to form a ring.
Rnd 1: Ch 1, work 6 sc in ring, join with sl st.
Rnd 2: Ch 2 (counts as 1 dc), work 3 dc in first (same) sc, 4 dc in each sc around — 24 dc, join with sl st to second ch of starting ch-2.
Rnd 3: Ch 1, skip first dc, work 1 sc in each of next 2 dc, skip next dc, *3 sc in sp between this 4-dc group and next 4-dc group, skip next dc, 1 sc in second and third dc of next 4-dc group, skip next dc, rep from * around, work 3 sc in last sp between two 4-dc groups, join with sl st to first st.
Rnd 4: Ch 1 and, starting in first sc of previous rnd, *work 1 sc in each of next 2 sc, skip 1 sc, 3 sc in center sc of next 3-sc group, skip next sc, rep from * around, join with sl st to first st. Fasten off.

Subsequent Hexagons: Work first 3 rnds as for basic hexagon and join on Rnd 4 as follows: Ch 1 and, starting in first sc of previous rnd, work 1 sc in each of next 2 sc, skip next sc, 1 sc in next corner sc, insert hook in same sc, and, holding right sides together of hexagons to be joined, insert hook in center corner sc on first hexagon and work 1 sc through both sts; insert hook in same sc on second hexagon and work 1 sc through next sc on first hexagon, (insert hook in next sc on second hexagon and work 1 sc in next sc on first hexagon) twice, skip 1 sc on second hexagon, (insert hook in next sc on second hexagon and join with sc to next sc on first hexagon) twice, 1 sc in same sc on second hexagon (do not join); complete Rnd 4 as for basic hexagon. Fasten off.

89

Components: Look at each component diagram carefully to determine the number of sides on which each hexagon must be joined. Keep in mind that the center corner sc sts will be shared by all the hexagons that meet at that point.

Component 1: Make 1.
Component 2: Make 6.
Component 3: Make 6.
Component 4: Make 2.
Component 5: Make 2.

Finishing: After all components have been completed, sew or sl st them together on wrong side of work, arranging them as shown on placement diagram.

#20 MOSAIC

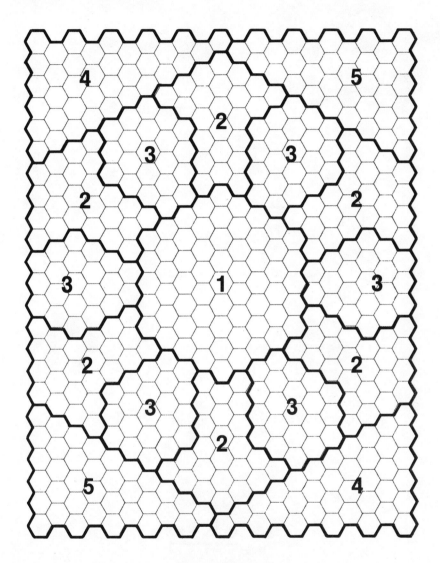

Placement Diagram

#20 MOSAIC

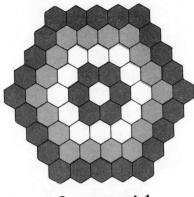

Component 1

Component 2

Component 3

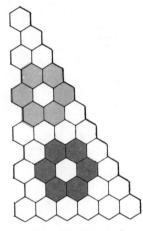

Component 4

Component 5

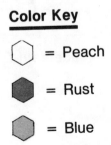

Color Key

⬡ = Peach

⬣ = Rust

⬣ = Blue

21 / Lone Ring

Approximate Finished Size: 42 by 54 inches
Average Experience Needed

Lone Ring is also known as Love Ring and Nonesuch. An amazing number of variations on this pattern can be achieved by changing the placement and color of the squares. The pattern is never-ending — it can be carried on for any number of rings you desire. Our crocheted afghan, which makes ideal "carry-along" work, is warm and cozy in shades of rust and green.

Materials:

Columbia-Minerva Wintuk 100% Du Pont Orlon acrylic, 4-ounce balls (knitting worsted weight):

   3 balls color 5734, olive
   2 balls color 5918, light beige
   2 balls color 5711, copperglo (rust)
   2 balls color 5733, medium olive
   1 ball color 5709, light copperglo (peach)

Crochet hook, size I, or size required to crochet to gauge
Yarn needle

Gauge: 3 double crochet = 1 inch; 3 rows = 2 inches

Note: Forty-eight squares make up this afghan. Each is worked in the same manner but in different two-color combinations. Work the first 5 rows in the first color listed below and the remainder of the square in the second color. Turning ch-2 counts as 1 dc.

Square A: Make 8 with light copperglo and copperglo.

Square B: Make 12 with medium olive and olive.

Square C: Make 8 with light beige and light copperglo.

Square D: Make 12 with copperglo and medium olive.

Square E: Make 8 with olive and light beige.

Squares:

Row 1: Ch 4, work 2 dc in fourth ch from hook—3 dc. Ch 2 and turn.

Row 2: Work 1 dc in first dc, 2 dc in each of next 2 dc—6 dc. Ch 2 and turn.

Row 3: Skip first dc, 2 dc in next dc, * 1 dc in next dc, 2 dc in next dc, rep from * across—9 dc. Ch 2 and turn.

Row 4: Skip first dc, 1 dc in next dc, 2 dc in next dc, *1 dc in each of next 2 dc, 2 dc in next dc, rep from * across—12 dc. Ch 2 and turn.

Row 5: Skip first dc, 1 dc in each of next 2 dc, 2 dc in next dc, *1 dc in each of next 3 dc, 2 dc in next dc, rep from * across—15 dc; remove last 2 lps of last dc with second color. Ch 2 and turn.

Row 6: With second color and working through back lps only, work across in dc, inc 1 dc in every fifth dc—18 dc. Ch 2 and turn.

Row 7: Working through both lps, work across in dc, inc 1 dc in every sixth dc—21 dc. Ch 2 and turn.

Row 8: Work across in dc, inc 1 dc in every seventh dc—24 dc. Ch 2 and turn.

Row 9: Work across in dc, inc 1 dc in every eighth dc—27 dc. Ch 2 and turn.

Row 10: Work across in dc, inc 1 dc in every ninth dc—30 dc. Turn.

Shape Square:

Row 1: Work 1 st in each st across as follows: 5 sl sts, 3 sc, 1 hdc, 12 dc, 1 hdc, 3 sc, 1 sl st. Turn.

Row 2: In same manner, work across as follows: skip first sl st, 4 sl sts, 3 sc, 1 hdc, 4 dc, 1 hdc, 3 sc, 1 sl st. Turn.

Row 3: Skip first sl st, work 2 sl sts, 2 sc, 1 hdc, 2 dc, 1 hdc, 2 sc, 1 sl st. Turn.

Row 4: Skip first sl st, work 3 sl sts, 4 dc tog (work 1 dc in each of next 4 sts, leaving last lp of each st on hook, yo, draw through all loops on hook). Fasten off.

Finishing: Work 1 row of color-over-color sc around each square, working 3 sc in each corner and 17 sc on each side. Following the placement diagram, sew the squares together. With olive, work 4 rows sc around entire joined piece, working 3 sc in each corner.

#21 LONE RING

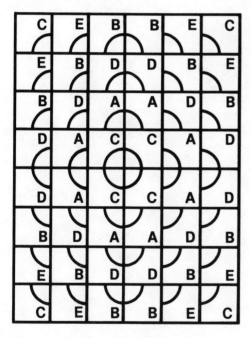

Placement Diagram

**See text for
square color explanation**

22 / Bridal Wreath

Approximate Finished Size: 45 by 56 inches
No Experience Needed

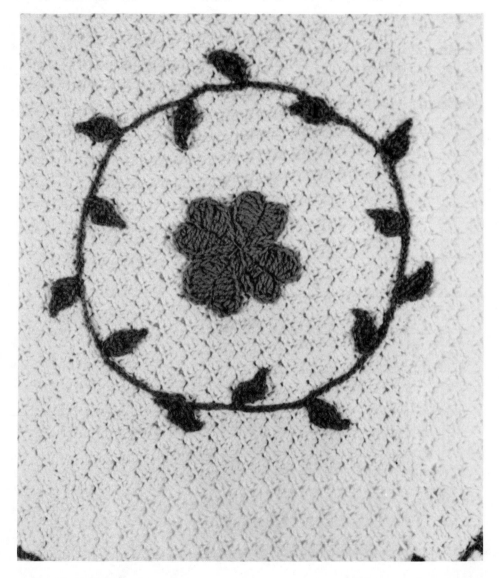

The Bridal Wreath quilt is one of many types of wedding quilt, usually
sewn at quilting parties, made to be given to the future couple. In many
versions of these quilts, particularly the Pennsylvania Dutch and those of
the Midwest and South, hearts symbolized the celebration of marriage.
In the afghan version of this design, the hearts create four-petaled
flowers wreathed in green and placed on a natural white background.

Materials:
Pingouin Le Yarn 2, 100-gram (3½-ounce) skeins (knitting worsted weight):
   13 skeins color 03, natural
   1 skein color 08, vermilion
   2 skeins color 58, bright green
Crochet hook, size I, or size required to crochet to gauge
Yarn needle

Gauge in Pattern Stitch: 3 stitches = 1 inch

Strips: Make 3. With natural, ch 44 loosely.
Row 1: Ch 1, 1 sc in second ch from hook, 2 dc in same ch, *skip 2 ch, (1 sc, 2 dc) in next ch — shell made; rep from * across, ending skip 2 ch, 1 sc in last ch. Ch 1 and turn.
Row 2: *1 shell in next sc, skip 2 dc; rep from * across, ending 1 sc in last sc. Ch 1 and turn.
Rep Row 2 for pat. Work even until piece measures 56 inches from beg.

Hearts: Make 20. With vermilion, ch 8. Work 3 tr in third ch from hook, 2 tr in next ch, 1 dc in next ch, 1 hdc in next ch, 1 sc in next ch, 2 sl sts in next ch; working along opposite edge of foundation ch, skip ch just worked in, work 1 st in each following ch, unless otherwise specified, as follows: 1 sc, 1 hdc, 1 dc, 2 tr in next ch, 3 tr in next ch, ch 2, 1 sl st in first ch. Fasten off.

Wreaths: Make 5. *Make stem:* With green, *ch 18. *Make leaf:* Starting in second ch from hook, work 1 st in each of next 8 ch as follows: 1 sl st, 1 sc, 1 hdc, 1 tr, 1 tr, 1 dc, 1 sc, 1 sl st. Turn. Rep from * fourteen times, turning only at the end of every second leaf so that the leaves will be positioned on both sides of the wreaths. Fasten off.

Finishing: Sew strips together. Form the wreaths into 12-inch rings and sew them in place, positioning one at the top and one at the bottom of each outer strip and one in the center of the middle strip. Sew four hearts in the center of each wreath, to make a four-petal flower, as shown in the photograph. With natural, work 1 row of sc around entire joined piece, working 3 sc in each corner. Finish with 2 rows sc in green worked in the same manner.

23/ Canopy

Approximate Finished Size: 43 by 50 inches
Experience Needed

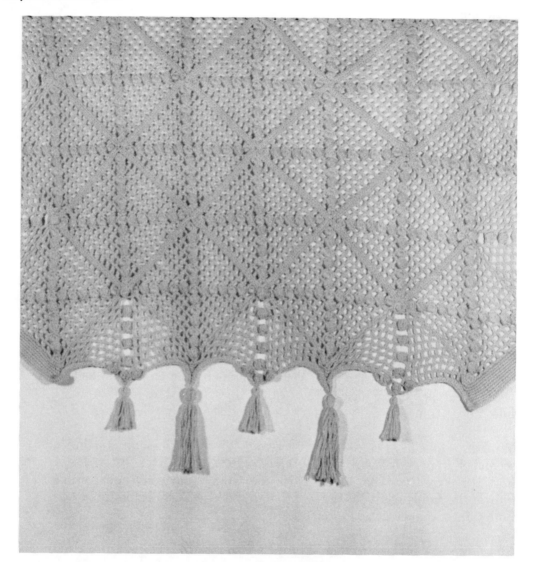

Although this afghan was not based on a quilt design, it was inspired by colonial times — by the net canopies that hung over tester beds. These can still be seen in many historic homes throughout New England. Many of the canopies were plain net mesh fringed all around, whereas others featured elaborate popcorn and tassel designs. The crocheted Canopy afghan here is an amalgam of both, made of eighteen simple squares joined diamond fashion. A border was then worked around the edge, each point of which was hung with a tassel. A beautiful natural wool was used to work the piece in order to heighten the antique effect.

Materials:
Pingouin Fleur de Laine, 100-gram (3½-ounce) skeins (knitting worsted weight):
  13 skeins undyed (natural)
Crochet hook, size G, or size required to crochet to gauge
Yarn needle

Gauge: 4 triple crochet = 1 inch; each square = approximately 9 inches

Note: To make popcorn st: Work 6 tr in same lp or ch, as specified, leaving last lp of each tr on hook, yo, draw through all lps on hook, ch 1 to fasten.

Squares: Make 18. Ch 43.
Row 1: Work 1 popcorn st in fifth ch from hook, skip 1 ch, 1 tr in next ch, (ch 2, skip 2 ch, 1 tr in next ch) eleven times, skip 1 ch, 1 popcorn in next ch, 1 tr in last ch. Ch 5 and turn.
Row 2: Skip first tr and popcorn, 1 tr in next tr, 1 popcorn in next ch-2 lp, 1 tr in next tr, (ch 2, 1 tr in next tr) nine times, 1 popcorn in next ch-2 lp, 1 tr in next tr, ch 2, 1 tr in third ch of turning ch-5. Ch 5 and turn.
Row 3: Skip first tr, 1 tr in next tr, ch 2, 1 tr in next tr, 1 popcorn in next ch-2 lp, 1 tr in next tr, (ch 2, 1 tr) seven times, 1 popcorn in next ch-2 lp, 1 tr in next tr, (ch 2, 1 tr) twice, working last tr in third ch of turning ch-5. Ch 5 and turn.
Row 4: Skip first tr, 1 tr in next tr, (ch 2, 1 tr in next tr) twice, 1 popcorn in next ch-2 lp, 1 tr in next tr, (ch 2, 1 tr in next tr) five times, 1 popcorn in next ch-2 lp, 1 tr in next tr, (ch 2, 1 tr in next tr) three times, working last tr in third ch of turning ch-5. Ch 5 and turn.
Row 5: Skip first tr, 1 tr in next tr, (ch 2, 1 tr in next tr) three times, 1 popcorn in next ch-2 lp, 1 tr in next tr, (ch 2, 1 tr in next tr) three times, 1 popcorn in next ch-2 lp, 1 tr in next tr, (ch 2, 1 tr in next tr) four times, working last tr in third ch of turning ch-5. Ch 5 and turn.
Row 6: Skip first tr, 1 tr in next tr, (ch 2, 1 tr in next tr) four times, 1 popcorn in next ch-2 lp, 1 tr in next tr, ch 2, 1 tr in next tr, 1 popcorn in next ch-2 lp, 1 tr in next tr, (ch 2, 1 tr in next tr) five times, working last tr in third ch of turning ch-5. Ch 5 and turn.
Row 7: Skip first tr, 1 tr in next tr, (ch 2, 1 tr in next tr) five times, 1 popcorn in next ch-2 lp, 1 tr in next tr, (ch 2, 1 tr in next tr) six times, working last tr in third ch of turning ch-5. Ch 5 and turn.
Row 8: Work as for Row 6.
Row 9: Work as for Row 5.
Row 10: Work as for Row 4.
Row 11: Work as for Row 3.

Row 12: Work as for Row 2.

Row 13: Work 1 popcorn in first ch-2 sp, 1 tr in next tr, (ch 2, 1 tr in next tr) eleven times, 1 popcorn in next ch-2 sp, 1 tr in third ch of turning ch-5. Fasten off.

Finishing: Work 1 row of sc around each square, working 38 sc along each side edge and 3 sc in each corner. Sew squares together as shown on placement diagram.

Border: When border is being worked, the sl sts at each point will cause the work to curl; this is the desired effect.

Row 1: Join yarn in center sc of corner of square indicated on placement diagram, work 3 sc in same sc, **1 sc in each of next sc across to next corner sc, 3 sc in same sc, [*(ch 5, skip 3 sc, 1 sc in next sc) nine times along side of next square, ch 2, 1 popcorn in intersection of three squares, ch 2, skip 3 sc along side of next square, 1 sc in next sc, (ch 5, skip 3 sc, 1 sc in next sc) eight times, ch 5, 3 sc in next corner sc], rep from * twice more, 1 sc in each of next sc across to next corner sc, 3 sc in same sc, rep portion between brackets twice more, rep from ** once more, ending last rep with ch 5 and 1 sl st to first sc (do not work 3 sc in 1 sc on last rep).

Row 2: Ch 1, work 3 sc in center sc of 3-sc group, 1 sc in each sc across to next center sc of 3-sc group, 3 sc in same sc, **[sl st in next sc, *1 sl st in each of next 3 ch, (ch 5, 1 sc in third ch of next ch-5 lp) eight times, ch 5, skip popcorn, 1 sc in third ch of next ch-5 lp, (ch 5, 1 sc in third ch of next ch-5 lp) eight times, 1 sl st in each of next 3 ch, 1 sl st in next sc, 3 sc in center sc of next 3-sc group], rep from * twice more, 1 sc in each sc across to next corner sc, 3 sc in next sc, rep portion between brackets twice more, rep from ** once more, ending last rep with 1 sl st in next sc; join with sl st to first st.

Row 3: Ch 1, 3 sc in next sc, **1 sc in each sc across to next center sc of 3-sc group, 3 sc in next sc, [*1 sl st in next sc, 1 sl st in each of next 3 sl sts, 1 sl st in each of next 2 ch on next ch-5 lp, 1 sc in next ch, (ch 5, 1 sc in third ch of next ch-5 lp) seven times, ch 2, 1 popcorn in center ch of next ch-5 lp, ch 2, 1 sc in third ch of next ch-5 lp, (ch 5, 1 sc in third ch of next ch-5 lp) seven times, 1 sl st in each of next 2 ch, 1 sl st in each of next sl sts to center sc of next 3-sc group, 3 sc in next sc], rep from * twice more, 1 sc in each sc across to next corner sc, 3 sc in next sc, rep portion between brackets twice more, rep from ** once more, ending last rep with 1 sl st in next sc, and join with sl st to first st.

Continue to work in this manner for 6 more rows, alternating Rows 2 and 3 but dec the number of ch-5 lps and inc the number of sl sts on each row by working 2 sl sts and 1 sc along the first 3 ch of first and last ch-5 lps on each side of popcorns. (Last row should have one popcorn remaining with one ch-5 lp on either side of it. Fasten off.

Popcorn Points: Make 10 points. Join yarn in sc before ch-5 preceding a popcorn on Row 9 of border.

Row 1: Ch 5, work 1 popcorn in third ch of ch-5 lp, ch 2, 1 tr in next sc, ch

5, 1 tr in next sc, ch 2, 1 popcorn in third ch of ch-5 lp, 1 tr in next sc. Ch 5 and turn.

Row 2: Work 1 popcorn in third ch of next ch-5 lp and 1 tr in next popcorn. Fasten off.

Large Tassels: Make 6. Cut thirty 15-inch strands of yarn and tie in the center with a 7-inch strand. Fold the strands in half at the tie, wrap one end of one of the strands securely around the folded strands 1 inch below the tie, fasten off, and trim the ends evenly.

Small Tassels: Make 10. Cut fifteen 8-inch strands of yarn and make tassels in same way as large tassels.

Fasten large tassels in sl-st points and small tassels in popcorn points.

#23 CANOPY

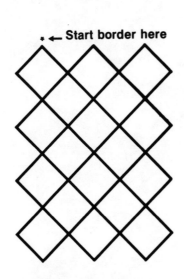

Placement Diagram

24/ Rose of Sharon

Approximate Finished Size: 47 by 55 inches
Experience Needed

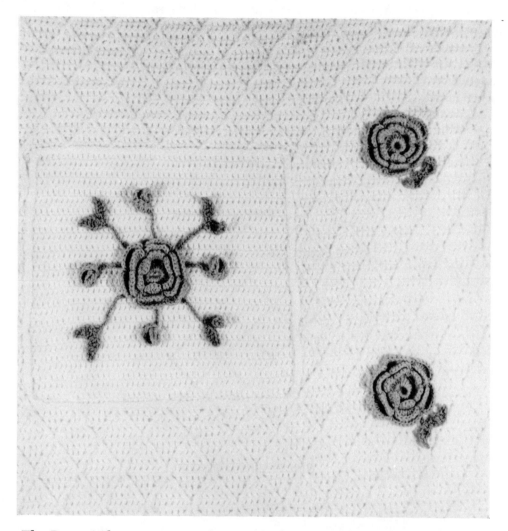

The Rose of Sharon is as popular a quilt design as any ever created. The rose has always been a favorite American garden flower, from the time of the early colonial gardens. Many variations of this traditionally pink-and-white quilt can be found, but for this crocheted afghan a highly textured diamond pattern has been used as a background for the three-dimensional roses that dot the piece. This afghan has a very warm and traditional beauty. (See p. 13 for a photograph of a Rose of Sharon quilt.)

Materials:
Phildar Leader, 100-gram (3½-ounce) balls (knitting worsted weight):
    12 balls color 10, white
     1 ball color 03, opaline green
     1 ball color 05, empire rose
Crochet hook, size I, or size required to crochet to gauge
Yarn needle

Gauge: 10 double crochet = 3 inches; 2 rows = 1 inch

Note: To work Front Post dc (FPdc), work as for dc, but instead of inserting hook into st, insert hook from front to back to front (working from right to left) around vertical post of dc on row below. To work Back Post dc (BPdc), work as for FPdc, but insert hook from back to front to back (working from right to left) around post of dc on row below. As these stitches are worked, a raised diagonal line will be formed on the right side of the work; the stitches forming this line are referred to in the instructions as diagonal dc.

Quilted-Pattern Stitch Section (Multiple of 8 plus 1): With white, ch 131 loosely.
Row 1: Starting in fourth ch from hook, work 1 dc in each ch across (ch-3 at beg of row counts as 1 dc) — 129 dc. Ch 2 and turn.
Row 2 (right side): Skip first dc of previous row, work 1 dc in each of next 2 dc, *skip next dc, work 1 FPdc around next dc, 1 dc in top of same dc, 1 FPdc around same dc, skip 1 dc, 1 dc in each of next 5 dc; rep from * across, ending skip next dc, work 1 FPdc around next dc, 1 dc in top of same dc, 1 FPdc around same dc, skip 1 dc, 1 dc in each of next 2 dc, 1 dc in turning ch (hereafter, the turning ch is referred to as a regular dc st). Ch 2 and turn.
Row 3: Skip first dc of previous row, 1 dc in next dc, *skip next dc, 1 BPdc around next diagonal dc, 1 dc in each of next 3 dc (including diagonal dc just worked), 1 BPdc around next diagonal dc (this will be the post of the same dc in which the last dc was just worked), skip next dc, 1 dc in each of next 3 dc; rep from * across, ending 1 dc in each of last 2 dc. Ch 2 and turn.
Row 4: Skip first 2 dc, *1 FPdc around next diagonal dc, 1 dc in each of next 5 dc (including the diagonal dc just worked), 1 FPdc around next diagonal dc, skip next dc, 1 dc in next dc, skip next dc; rep from * across, ending 1 dc in last dc. Ch 2 and turn.
Row 5: *1 BPdc around next diagonal dc, 1 dc in each of next 7 dc (including the diagonal dc just worked), 1 BPdc around next diagonal dc, skip next dc; rep from * across, ending 1 dc in last dc. Ch 2 and turn.

103

Row 6: 1 FPdc around next diagonal dc, *skip 1 dc, 1 dc in each of next 5 dc, skip 1 dc, skip next diagonal dc, 1 FPdc around next diagonal dc, 1 dc between 2 diagonal dc of previous row, 1 FPdc around skipped diagonal dc; rep from * across, ending skip 1 dc, 1 dc in each of next 5 dc, skip 1 dc, 1 FPdc around next diagonal dc, 1 dc in last dc. Ch 2 and turn.

Row 7: Skip first dc, 1 dc in next dc, 1 BPdc around next diagonal dc, *skip 1 dc, 1 dc in each of next 3 dc, skip 1 dc, 1 BPdc around next diagonal dc, 1 dc in each of next 3 dc (including the diagonal dc just worked), 1 BPdc around next diagonal dc; rep from * across, ending skip 1 dc, 1 dc in each of next 3 dc, skip 1 dc, 1 BPdc around next diagonal dc, 1 dc in last 2 dc, including diagonal dc just worked. Ch 2 and turn.

Row 8: Skip first dc, 1 dc in each of next 2 dc, 1 FPdc around next diagonal dc, *skip 1 dc, 1 dc in next dc, skip 1 dc, 1 FPdc around next diagonal dc, 1 dc in each of next 5 dc (including last diagonal dc worked), 1 FPdc around next diagonal dc; rep from * across, ending skip 1 dc, 1 dc in next dc, skip 1 dc, 1 FPdc around next diagonal dc, 1 dc in each of last 3 dc, including last diagonal dc worked. Ch 2 and turn.

Row 9: Skip first dc, 1 dc in each of next 3 dc, *1 BPdc around next diagonal dc, skip 1 dc, 1 BPdc around next diagonal dc, 1 dc in each of next 7 dc (including diagonal dc just worked), rep from * across, ending 1 BPdc around next diagonal dc, skip next dc, 1 BPdc around next diagonal dc, 1 dc in each of next 4 dc (including diagonal dc just worked). Ch 2 and turn.

Row 10: Skip first dc, 1 dc in each of next 2 dc, *skip 1 dc, skip next diagonal dc, 1 FPdc around next diagonal dc, 1 dc between 2 diagonal dc of previous row, 1 FPdc around skipped diagonal dc, skip 1 dc, 1 dc in each of next 5 dc; rep from * across, ending skip 1 dc, skip next diagonal dc, 1 FPdc around next diagonal dc, 1 dc between 2 diagonal dc of previous row, 1 FPdc around skipped diagonal dc, skip 1 dc, 1 dc in each of last 3 dc. Ch 2 and turn.

Rep Rows 3 through 10 for pat st. Work even in pat st for 37 rows (ending with a Row 5). Mark center 47 sts and work in dc only on those sts for 28 rows, maintaining sts on each outside edge in pat st. Return to pat st across all sts for 37 rows. Fasten off.

Border: With white, work 1 rnd of sc around entire piece, working 3 sc in each corner. Ch 1 and turn. Working through back lps only, work 19 more rnds of sc, working 3 sc in each corner; ch 1 and turn at end of each rnd. Fasten off.

Finishing: With doubled white yarn, make a chain approximately 56 inches long and sew it around the square of dc at center of afghan.

Roses: Make 9. With rose, ch 8 and join with sl st to form a ring.
Rnd 1: Ch 2 (counts as 1 dc), work 17 dc in ring, and join with sl st to first st.
Rnd 2: Work 1 sc in same st as sl st, *ch 4, skip 2 dc, 1 sc in next dc; rep from * around, ending ch 4, and join with sl st to first st.
Rnd 3: Work (1 sc, 5 dc, 1 sc) in each ch-4 lp around.

Rnd 4: Working behind petals of Rnd 3, *ch 5 and work 1 sc around next sc of Rnd 2; rep from * around, ending ch 5, and join with sl st to first st.
Rnd 5: Work (1 sc, 1 hdc, 5 dc, 1 hdc, 1 sc) in each ch-5 lp around.
Rnd 6: Working behind petals of Rnd 5, *ch 6 and work 1 sc around next sc of Rnd 4; rep from * around, ending ch 6, and join with sl st to first st.
Rnd 7: Work (1 sc, 1 hdc, 7 dc, 1 hdc, 1 sc) in each ch-6 lp around. Join with sl st to first st. Fasten off.

Center Rosebuds and Stems: Make 4. With rose, ch 4 and join with sl st to form a ring.
Rnd 1: Work 12 dc in ring. Ch 4 and turn.
Rnd 2: Skip first dc, 1 tr in each of next 2 dc, 1 dc in each of next 3 dc, 1 hdc in each of next 2 dc, 1 sc in each of next 2 dc, 1 sl st in each of next 2 sts. Fold this short edge of piece over long edge and join with a sl st to top back of fourth dc of Rnd 1. Fasten off.
Join green yarn at base of each rosebud and ch 12 to make stems. Fasten off.

Leaves: Make 8. With green, ch 12 and turn. *Work 1 sc in second ch from hook, 1 hdc in next ch, 1 dc in next ch, 1 tr in next ch, 1 dc in next ch, 1 sc in next ch*—first leaf made. Continuing, ch 7 and turn. Rep section between * and * and join with sl st to last sc at base of leaf.

Center Stems and Leaves: Make 4. With green, ch 19 and work as for leaves above.

Finishing: Sew one rose in the center of the framed dc square, surrounding it with the four rosebuds and their stems and the leaves with their stems (see photo). Space the remaining eight roses, each with a leaf sewn to it, around the center motif; sew in place.

25/ Dresden Plate

Approximate Finished Size: 48 by 62 inches
Average Experience Needed

*The Dresden Plate quilt is also known as the Aster or Friendship Ring.
The name Friendship Ring came from the fact that the "plates" were
made from scraps of many printed fabrics traded among friends. The
crocheted translation shown here has a three-dimensional aspect because
the "plate" edges stand out from the background. The bright colors of
the plates contrast strikingly with the black background.*

Materials:
Phildar Pégase, 50-gram (1¾-ounce) balls (knitting worsted weight):
   17 balls color 64, noir (black)
    3 balls color 96, véronèse (green)
    3 balls color 28, cerise (red)
    3 balls color 40, gauloise (blue)
    3 balls color 33, églantine (pink)
Crochet hook, size H, or size required to crochet to gauge
Yarn needle

Gauge: 3 double crochet = 1 inch

Note: When changing to a new color, work several sts over the clipped end of the previous color to avoid having to weave in ends when finishing the piece.

Squares: Make 20.
Center Circle: With black, ch 8 and join with sl st to form a ring.
Rnd 1: Ch 1 and work 8 sc in ring. Join with sl st to first st.
Rnd 2: Ch 1 and work 2 sc in each st around—16 sc; join with sl st to first st.
Rnd 3: Ch 2 (counts as 1 dc) and work around in dc, inc 1 st in every second st—24 dc; join with sl st to first st.
Rnd 4: Ch 2 (counts as 1 dc) and work around in dc, inc 1 st in every third dc—32 dc; join with sl st to first st and fasten off.

Outer Circle:
Color A: Join green in any st, ch 10, and turn. Starting in fifth ch from hook, work 1 dc in each of next 3 ch, 1 hdc in next ch, 1 sc in next ch, 1 sl st in same sc as joining of green, 1 sl st in next st on circle, turn. *Work 1 sc in next sc of same color, 1 hdc in next hdc, 1 dc in each of next 3 dc, 1 tr in fourth ch of turning ch-4. To make the scallop: Sl st back along edge of 2 rows just completed to first turning ch, turn and ch 1. Work (1 sc, 1 hdc, 1 dc) in sp created by turning ch-4, 1 tr in base of tr, and (1 dc, 1 hdc, 1 sc) around post of the tr, removing last 2 lps of last sc with red yarn.
Color B: With red, ch 4. Working through back lps only, work 1 dc in each of next 3 dc, 1 hdc in next hdc, 1 sc in next sc, (1 sl st in next black sc on circle) twice, turn. Complete this portion by working from * as for Color A, changing to blue on last sc. Fasten off.
Color C: With blue, work as for Color B, changing to pink on last sc.
Color D: With pink, work as for Color B.

Rep the four-color sequence three times more. Join last color to first color with a row of 5 sl sts on wrong side of work. Fasten off.

Shape Square:
Rnd 1: With black, join yarn to back of first sc on any color-A scallop. Working behind the scallop, *ch 5 and work 1 sc in back of first sc of next scallop; rep from * around, ending ch 5, and join with sl st to first sc.
Rnd 2: Work 5 sc in each ch-5 lp around and join with sl st to first st.
Rnd 3: Ch 2 (counts as 1 dc), skip first sc of previous rnd, work 1 dc in next dc, *3 dc in next dc — corner made; 1 dc in each of next 2 dc, 1 dc in each of next sc until center sc behind next green scallop has been reached; rep from * around. Join with sl st to first st.
Rnds 4 and 5: Work around in dc, working 3 dc in each center corner st.
Rnds 6 and 7: Working through back lps only, work in sc, working 3 sc through both lps in each center corner st. Fasten off.

Finishing: Block each square lightly. Sew squares together in a four-square-wide by five-square-long arrangement.

26/ Grandmother's Fan

Approximate Finished Size: 52 by 62 inches
Experience Needed

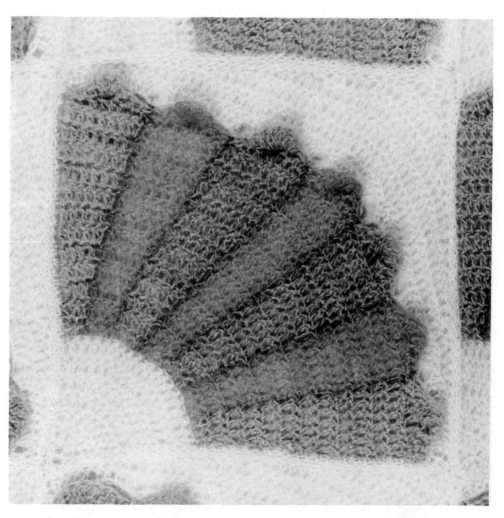

Grandmother's Fan, also known as Fanny's Fan, is similar to the
Dresden Plate design except that only one quarter of the patterned circle
is used to create the fan in each square. In many of the earliest quilts,
elaborate embroidery stitches were used to outline the fans and the
borders of the squares. The crocheted afghan translated from this design
has the added beauty of mohair yarn to give it a soft and fluffy texture.
A delicate scalloped border edging the afghan echoes the fan motif.

Materials:
Pingouin Mohair 70, 50-gram (1¾-ounce) balls (mohair):
    8 balls color 19, ecru (beige)
    3 balls color 10, cosmos (lavender)
    3 balls color 36, vert d'eau (turquoise)
    4 balls color 28, giroselle (gold)
Crochet hook, size H, or size required to crochet to gauge
Yarn needle

Gauge: 7 double crochet = 2 inches; 5 rows = 3 inches

Note: To change color in the middle of a row, remove last 2 lps of previous st with new color. To keep yarn from tangling, do not carry it along; use a separate ball for each color section. Place the balls, in order of use, on the floor around you. When going from row to row, turn the piece carefully to keep the strands in order.

Squares: Make 20. With beige, ch 4.
Row 1: Work 2 dc in fourth ch from hook—3 dc. Ch 2 (counts as 1 dc) and turn.
Row 2: Work 1 dc in first dc and 2 dc in each of next 2 dc—6 dc. Ch 2 and turn.
Row 3: Work 1 dc in first dc, *1 dc in next dc, 2 dc in next dc, rep from * across—9 dc. Ch 2 and turn.
Row 4: Skip first dc, 1 dc in next dc, 2 dc in next dc, *1 dc in each of next 2 dc, 2 dc in next dc, rep from * across—12 dc. Ch 2 and turn.
Row 5: Skip first dc, 1 dc in each of next 2 dc, 2 dc in next dc, *1 dc in each of next 3 dc, 2 dc in next dc, rep from * across—15 dc. Ch 2 and turn.
Row 6: Skip first dc, 1 dc in each of next 3 dc, 2 dc in next dc, *1 dc in each of next 4 dc, 2 dc in next dc, rep from * across—18 dc. Ch 2 and turn.
Row 7: Skip first dc, 1 dc in each of next 4 dc, 2 dc in next dc, *1 dc in each of next 5 dc, 2 dc in next dc, rep from * across—21 dc. Fasten off.
Row 8: Join lavender. Working 1 dc in each dc across, work 3 dc in lavender (ch 2 for first dc), 3 dc in gold, 3 dc in turquoise, 3 dc in gold, 3 dc in turquoise, 3 dc in gold, 3 dc in lavender—21 dc.
Row 9: Work in dc across, maintaining colors as established and inc 1 dc in center dc of each color group—28 dc. Ch 2 and turn.
Row 10: Work even, maintaining colors as established. Ch 2 and turn.
Row 11: Work in dc across, maintaining colors and inc 1 dc between 2 center dc of each color group—35 dc. Ch 2 and turn.
Row 12: Work even, maintaining colors.
Rep Rows 9 through 12; then rep Rows 9, 10, and 11—you should have 9 sts in each color group, for a total of 63 dc.

Scallop:
Row 1: Across each 9-st color group, work 1 sl st, 1 sc, 1 hdc, 1 dc, 1 tr, 1 dc, 1 hdc, 1 sc, 1 sl st. Ch 1 and turn.

Row 2: Across each color group, work 1 sl st, 1 sc, 1 hdc, 1 dc, 3 tr in next tr, 1 dc, 1 hdc, 1 sc, 1 sl st. Fasten off and turn.

Shape Square:
Row 1: Join beige and, starting in first sl st, work 1 sc in back of st, *ch 5, 1 sc (inserting hook in back lp at base of center tr so that beige cannot be seen on right side of work), ch 5, 1 sc in back lps of 2 sl sts at point of next color change; rep from * across, ending ch 5, 1 sc (inserting hook in back lp at base of center tr), ch 5, 1 sc in back of last sl st. Ch 2 (counts as 1 dc) and turn.
Row 2: Work 5 dc in each ch-5 lp across—70 dc.
Row 3: On this and all following rows, work 1 st in each st respectively as follows (be sure to work the sl sts loosely). Work 6 sl sts, 1 sc, 1 hdc, 54 dc, 1 hdc, 1 sc, 1 sl st, leaving last sts unworked; turn.
Row 4: Skip first sl st and work 6 sl sts, 1 sc, 1 hdc, 42 dc, 1 hdc, 1 sc, 1 sl st; turn.
Row 5: Skip first sl st and work 6 sl sts, 1 sc, 1 hdc, 30 dc, 1 hdc, 1 sc, 1 sl st; turn.
Row 6: Skip first sl st and work 4 sl sts, 1 sc, 1 hdc, 22 dc, 1 hdc, 1 sc, 1 sl st; turn.
Row 7: Skip first sl st and work 4 sl sts, 1 sc, 1 hdc, 17 dc, 1 hdc, 1 sc, 1 sl st; turn.
Row 8: Skip first sl st and work 3 sl sts, 1 sc, 1 hdc, 8 dc, 1 hdc, 1 sc, 1 sl st; turn.
Row 9: Skip first sl st and work 1 sl st, 1 sc, 1 hdc, 4 dc tog (work 1 dc in each of next 4 dc, leaving last lp of each dc on hook, yo, draw through all lps on hook), 1 hdc, 1 sc, 1 sl st.

Finishing: With beige, work 1 row of sc around each square, working 3 sc in each corner and 36 sc on each side. (Be sure to work the same number of sts on each side so that the piece will be square.) Sew the squares together in a four-square-wide by five-square-long arrangement, positioning each so that the fan is in the lower left corner.

Scallop Border:
With beige and right side of work facing, work around the edge of joined piece, working 1 st in each st respectively as follows. Work *1 sl st, 1 sc, 1 hdc, 1 dc, 5 tr in same st, 1 dc, 1 hdc, 1 sc; rep from * around, join with sl st to first st, and fasten off.

27 / Patchwork Puffs

Approximate Finished Size: 45 by 55 inches
No Experience Needed

This Patchwork Puffs afghan is based on the very simplest of all quilting techniques—the piecing together of patchwork squares. This procedure was just one step up from the Crazy Quilt designs, which combined multicolored scraps in a completely haphazard fashion. The organization of patchwork squares was the forerunner of the more elaborate designs to come. Because each square of this crocheted patchwork afghan is double-thickness, the piece can serve as a winter throw or even as a rug. If you wish to make a blanket lighter in weight, make the squares single-thickness.

Materials:
Reynolds Town and Country, 50-gram (1¾-ounce) balls (sport weight):
  10 balls, color 228 (light olive green)
  10 balls color 270 (mauve)
  10 balls color 248 (peach)
  10 balls color 216 (medium blue)
Crochet hook, size H, or size required to crochet to gauge
Yarn needle

Gauge in Pattern Stitch: 7 double crochet = 2 inches; 6 rows = 4½ inches

Note: Ch-2 at beg of each row counts as 1 dc. Each puff is a double-thickness square. To work the Front Post dc (FPdc), work as for dc, but instead of inserting hook into st, insert hook from front to back to front (working from right to left) around vertical post of dc on row below. To work Back Post dc (BPdc), work as for FPdc, but insert hook from back to front to back (working from right to left) around post of dc on row below.

Squares: Make 24 in light olive green and 25 each in mauve, peach, and medium blue. Ch 18 loosely.
Row 1: Starting in third ch from hook, work 1 dc in each ch across. Ch 2 and turn.
Row 2: Work across in FPdc, working first st around second dc of row below, and ending 1 dc in turning ch-2 of previous row. Ch 2 and turn.
Row 3: Work across in BPdc, working first st around second dc of row below, and ending 1 dc in turning ch-2 of previous row. Ch 2 and turn.
Rep Rows 2 and 3 twice more; then rep Row 3. Work Row 3 once again (by doing this, a ridge will be formed on the opposite side of the work—this is the folding line of the square). Now alternate Rows 2 and 3 twice more, rep Row 2 once, and work 1 row of regular dc; ch 1 and turn. Join beginning and ending edges of square by working 1 sc in each st across, working each sc through 2 sts at once. Continue around remaining edges of square, working through two thicknesses along both side edges to join them.

Finishing: Sew squares together, following placement diagram.

#27 PATCHWORK PUFFS

1	2	3	4	1	2	3	4	1
2	3	4	1	2	3	4	1	2
3	4	1	2	3	4	1	2	3
4	1	2	3	4	1	2	3	4
1	2	3	4	1	2	3	4	1
2	3	4	1	2	3	4	1	2
3	4	1	2	3	4	1	2	3
4	1	2	3	4	1	2	3	4
1	2	3	4	1	2	3	4	1
2	3	4	1	2	3	4	1	2
3	4	1	2	3	4	1	2	3

Placement Diagram

Color Key

1 = Peach

2 = Medium blue

3 = Mauve

4 = Light olive green

28 / North Carolina Lily

Approximate Finished Size: 48 by 75 inches
Average Experience Needed

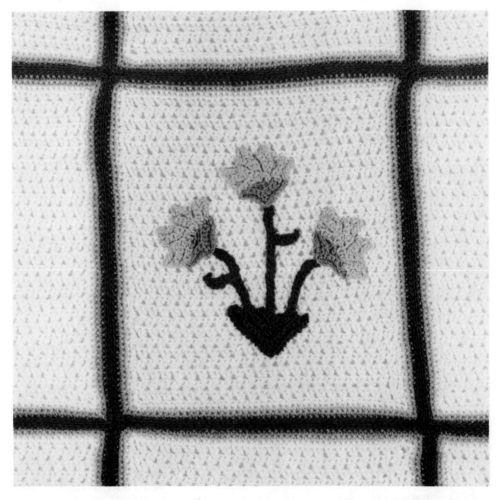

To make a North Carolina Lily quilt required considerable skill on the part of the worker. The flower portions of each patterned square were pieced separately, and then the entire plant was appliquéd on the diagonal to each square. Quilted, plain-colored squares were then sewn diamond fashion between the patterned squares. This crocheted afghan is a bit simpler to make, but it is just as attractive. Made of natural wools in traditional colors, it features lily plants worked separately and then appliquéd to the crocheted background squares. (See p. 14 for a photograph of a North Carolina Lily quilt.)

115

Materials:
Reynolds Lopi Light, 50-gram (1¾-ounce) balls (sport weight):
   22 balls color 401 (white)
    4 balls color 421 (dark green)
    3 balls color 423 (pink)
    3 balls color 413 (light green)
Crochet hook, size I, or size required to crochet to gauge
Yarn needle

Gauge in Pattern Stitch: 4 stitches = 1 inch; 3 rows = 2 inches

Pattern Stitch:
Make a chain of specified length.
Row 1: Ch 3, 1 dc in fifth ch from hook, 1 dc in fourth ch from hook, *skip 1 ch, 1 dc in next ch, 1 dc in skipped ch, rep from * across, and end 1 dc in last ch. Ch 3 and turn.
Row 2: *Skip 1 dc, 1 dc in next dc, 1 dc in skipped dc, rep from * across, and end 1 dc in last dc. Ch 3 and turn.
Rep Row 2 for pat.

Squares: Make 12. With white, ch 47. Work even in pat st for 27 rows. Fasten off.

Flowerpots: Make 6. With dark green, ch 24.
Row 1: Starting in second ch from hook, work 1 sc in each of next 11 ch, skip 1 ch, 1 sc in each of next 11 ch. Ch 1 and turn.
Row 2: Working through back lps only, skip first sc, 1 sc in each of next sc to center 2 sc, skip center 2 sc, 1 sc in each of next sc, skipping last sc. Ch 1 and turn. Rep Row 2 four times more. Do not fasten off.

Main Stem: Continuing with dark green, ch 19 and turn. Starting in second ch from hook, work 1 sc in each of next 18 ch, join with sl st to next sc in center of flowerpot, and fasten off.

Side Stems: Fasten dark green in end of third row of flowerpot. Ch 13 and turn. Work 1 sc in each of next 12 ch; join with sl st in fourth row on pot. Fasten off. Work another stem in same manner on other side of pot.

Leaves: Join dark green on left side of left-side stem in sixth st from flowerpot. Ch 6 and turn. Skipping first ch, work 1 sl st in next ch, 1 sc in next ch, 1 hdc in next ch, 1 dc in next ch, 1 sc in next ch, and join with sl st to starting st on stem. Fasten off. Rep on twelfth st on right side of main stem to make another leaf.

Lily Bases: Make 18. With light green, ch 14.
Row 1 (right side): Starting in second ch from hook, work 1 sc in each of next 6 ch, skip 1 ch, 1 sc in each of next 6 ch. Ch 1 and turn.
Rows 2 and 3: Work as for Row 2 of flowerpot. Fasten off.

Lilies: Make 18, using lily bases just completed.

First Petal:
Row 1: With wrong side of lily base facing and using pink, work 1 sc in each of the first 3 rows and 1 sc in first of center 2 sc. Ch 1 and turn.
Row 2: Working through back lps and skipping first sc, work 1 sc in each of next 2 sc and 2 sc in next sc. Ch 1 and turn.
Row 3: Work 1 sc in each of next 4 sc. Ch 1 and turn.
Row 4: Rep Row 2.
Row 5: Work 1 sl st in each of next 4 sts.

Second Petal:
Row 1: Continuing, work 3 sc along edge of petal just completed and 1 sc in same green st as fourth pink sc on Row 1 of first petal.
Rows 2 through 5: Work Rows 2, 3, 4, and 5 of first petal.

Third Petal: Continuing, work as for second petal, working last sc of Row 1 into first sc to left of center. Work Rows 2, 3, 4, and 5.

Fourth Petal: Continuing, work as for third petal, working last sc of Row 1 into second sc to left of center and working a sl st to join to flowerpot at end of each of Rows 3 and 5. Fasten off.

Finishing: Using white, then pink, light green, and dark green, work 1 rnd of sc in each color around each square, working 3 sc in each corner. Sew lilies to the centers of six of the squares. Sew the squares together, alternating the decorated squares with the plain ones, in a three-square-wide by four-square-long arrangement. Work 1 row of sc in dark green around entire joined piece, working 3 sc in each corner.

5

Crocheted Lap Robes

29/ Star of Bethlehem

Approximate Finished Size: 43 by 43 inches
Experience Needed

Traditionally fashioned in blue and white, the Star of Bethlehem quilt is also known as the Prairie Star, Harvest Star, Lone Star, and Ship's Wheel. The patience required to piece together the tiny diamond-shaped pieces of fabric characteristic of this pattern is truly mind-boggling. For this crocheted lap robe, the diamonds were added in rounds, one color at a time, and the background was made separately. The colors chosen were unusual, and the yarn, a mohair/wool/acrylic mixture, was worked in ridges of single crochet to give the piece more texture. (See p. 15 for a photograph of a Star of Bethlehem quilt.)

Materials:

Pingouin Orage, 50-gram (1¾-ounce) balls (mohair/wool/acrylic):

    2 balls color 119, prusse (dark blue): Color A

    2 balls color 117, lande (light green): Color B

    3 balls color 121, bordeaux (dark purple): Color C

    2 balls color 142, lilas (light purple): Color D

    10 balls color 136, aube (peach): Color E

Crochet hook, size H, or size required to crochet to gauge

Yarn needle

Gauge: 7 single crochet = 2 inches; 5 rows = 2 inches

Note: Work in sc through back lps only throughout unless otherwise specified.

Center Star:

Color A:

First Point: Ch 9.

Row 1 (wrong side): Starting in second ch from hook, work 1 sc in each ch across—8 sc. Ch 1 and turn.

Row 2: Skipping first sc, work 1 sc in each of next 6 sc and 2 sc in last sc—8 sc. Ch 1 and turn.

Row 3: Work 2 sc in first sc and 1 sc in each of next 6 sc—8 sc. Ch 1 and turn.

Row 4: Work as for Row 2.

Row 5: Work as for Row 3.

Row 6: Work as for Row 2.

Row 7: Work as for Row 3, except after ch-1 at end of row, do not turn.

Second Point:

Row 1 (wrong side): Work 1 sc in end of each of previous 7 rows. Ch 1 and turn.

Row 2: Skipping first sc, work 1 sc in each of next 6 sc and 2 sc in ch-1 at end of Row 7 on first point—8 sc. Ch 1 and turn.

Row 3: Work 2 sc in first sc and 1 sc in each of next 6 sc—8 sc. Ch 1 and turn.

Row 4: Skipping first sc, work 1 sc in each of next 6 sc and 2 sc in last sc—8 sc. Ch 1 and turn.

Row 5: Work as for Row 3.

Row 6: Work as for Row 4.

Row 7: Work as for Row 3, except after ch-1 at end of row, do not turn.

Third, Fourth, Fifth, Sixth, and Seventh Points:

Work as for second point.

Eighth Point:

Work as for second point. After working Row 7, join to first point by working 1 sl st in end of each of previous 7 rows, at the same time working these sl sts through ch sts along bottom edge of foundation ch on first point. Fasten off.

Color B:

First Point:

Row 1: With wrong side of work facing, join B and work 1 sc in sc at tip of any point, and work 1 sc in each of 8 sc across. Ch 1 and turn.

Rows 2, 4, and 6: Work as for Row 2 on other points.

Rows 3 and 5: Work as for Row 3 on other points.

Row 7: Work as for Row 7 on other points.

Second Point:

Row 1 (wrong side): Work 1 sc in end of each of previous 7 rows. Being sure to work sl sts so that they are not visible on right side of work, work 1 sl st in end of first row of adjacent Color A point and 1 sl st in end of next row on same point. Ch 1 and turn.

Row 2: Skipping first sc, work 1 sc in each of next 6 sc and 2 sc in turning ch-1. Ch 1 and turn.

Rows 3 and 5: Work as for Row 3 on other points. At end of row, insert hook in next same-color sc and join end of row to corresponding row of Color A point by making a sl st through all 3 lps on hook; advance to the next row on same point with a sl st, joining on wrong side of work. Do not ch 1. Turn.

Rows 4 and 6: Work as for Row 2 on other points.

Row 7: Work as for Row 7 on other points and join with sl st to corresponding row on next point, first inserting hook in last sc of previous row. Rep first and second points seven times more around.

Color C:

With wrong side of work facing, join C in sc at tip of any point 1. *Work point 1 and point 2 in first angle as before. Work point 2 only in next angle. Rep from * seven times more, joining last point to first point as before.

Color D:

With wrong side of work facing, join D in sc at tip of any point 1. *Work points 1 and 2 in first angle, and work point 2 only in each of next two angles; rep from * seven times more, joining end of rnd as before.

Shape Points of Star: *Join Color A in sc at tip of point 2 worked immediately after a point 1. Referring to diagram, work point 2 in this and each of next two angles, fasten off, and rep from * seven times more. Join Color B in sc at tip of first point of three point-2 groups, work a point 2 in each of next two angles, and fasten off; rep for remaining seven points. Join Color C in sc at tip of first point of two point-2 pairs, work a point 2 in angle between this and next point, and fasten off; rep for remaining seven points.

Corner Pieces: Make 4. With E, ch 41. Starting in second ch from hook, sc through back lps only for 38 rows. Fasten off.

Side Triangles: Make 4. With E, ch 4.

Row 1: Starting in second ch from hook and working in sc through back lps only, work 1 sc in each ch — 3 sc. Ch 1 and turn.

Row 2: Inc 1 st in each sc — 6 sc. Ch 1 and turn.

Row 3: Inc 1 st in each of first 2 sc, work in sc to last sc, and work 2 sc in last st. Ch 1 and turn. Rep last row until there are 60 sc — 20 rows in all. Work even in back lps only for 10 more rows. Fasten off.

Finishing: Sew one corner piece in every second angle between points of star, making sure that the rows of sc all run in the same direction. Fit one side triangle in each remaining angle between points and sew in place. With E, work 1 row sc around entire joined piece, working 3 sc in each corner. Fasten off. With C and working through back lps only, work in sc around, working 3 sc in each corner. Fasten off.

#29 STAR OF BETHLEHEM

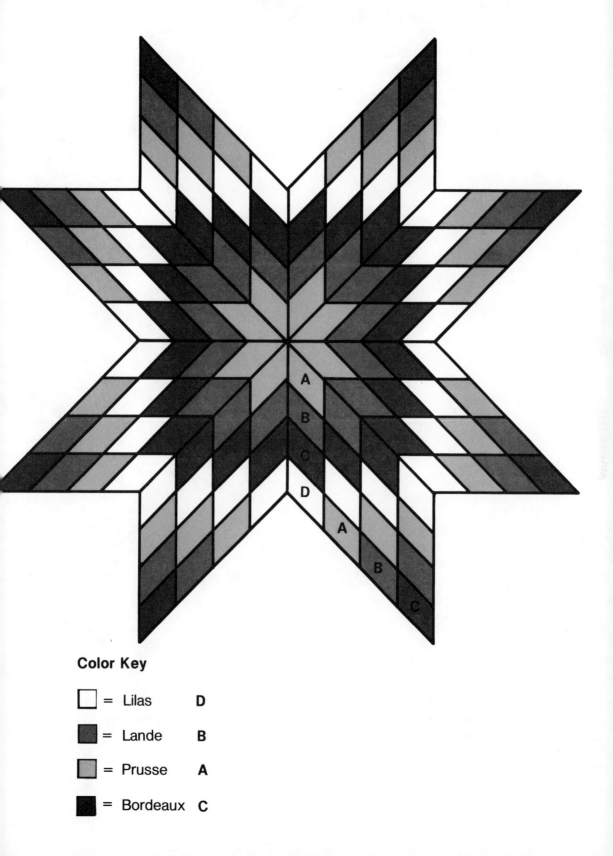

Color Key

☐ = Lilas   **D**

■ = Lande   **B**

■ = Prusse   **A**

■ = Bordeaux   **C**

30/ Zigzag

Approximate Finished Size: 40 by 50 inches
No Experience Needed

Zigzag is a variation of the Brick Wall motif. An ideal beginner's pattern for both quilter and crocheter, it can be left with the angles free at the edges, as we've done, or the angles can be pieced to fill them out. The pieced rectangles could also be appliquéd onto a solid backing.

Materials:

Coats & Clark Red Heart 4-ply hand-knitting yarn, 99.2 gram (3½-ounce) skeins (knitting worsted weight):

   3 skeins color 1, white

   3 skeins color 810, Yale blue

   3 skeins color 681, mist green

   2 skeins color 737, pink

Crochet hook, size I, or size required to crochet to gauge

Yarn needle

Gauge in Pattern Stitch: 11 stitches = 3 inches; 4 rows = 1 inch

Rectangles: Make 14 white, 14 blue, 14 green, and 7 pink. Ch 34 loosely.
Row 1: Work 1 sc in fourth ch from hook, *ch 1, skip 1 ch, 1 sc in next ch, rep from * across. Ch 2 and turn.
Row 2: *Work 1 sc in next ch-1 sp, ch 1, rep from * across, ending 1 sc in turning ch of previous row. Ch 2 and turn.
Rep Row 2 fourteen times more for pat. Fasten off.

Finishing: Sew rectangles together, following diagram for placement.

#30 ZIGZAG

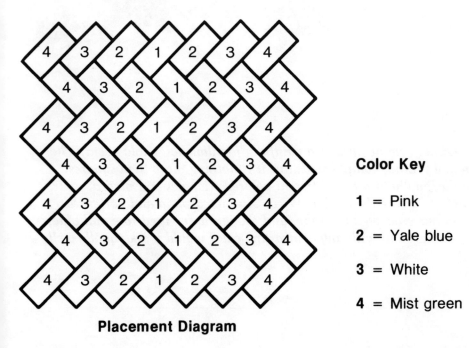

Color Key

1 = Pink

2 = Yale blue

3 = White

4 = Mist green

Placement Diagram

31 / Broken Dishes

Approximate Finished Size: 40 by 50 inches
Average Experience Needed

Broken Dishes commemorates a painfully familiar household event. The pattern looks rather complicated, but it is nothing more than squares divided diagonally into two different-colored triangles and placed alternately to create the design. We've alternated plain and patterned squares in our crocheted lap robe, and though we've used rose and blue, a white background with any contrasting color would work equally well.

Materials:
Phildar Pégase, 50-gram (1¾-ounce) balls (knitting worsted weight):
  12 balls color 23, ciel (light blue)
   8 balls color 53, lupin (rose)
Crochet hook, size H, or size required to crochet to gauge
Yarn needle

Gauge: 6 single crochet = 2 inches; 7 rows = 2 inches

Note: To change colors in middle of row, remove last 2 lps of last st with new color; do not carry old color along under new color.

Plain Squares: Make 6. With light blue, ch 41. Work even in sc on 40 sts for 40 rows. Fasten off.

Patterned Squares: Make 6, each of which is composed of 4 small squares (24 small squares in all).
Small Square — Part 1: With rose, ch 11.
Row 1 (right side): Starting in second ch from hook, work 1 sc in each of next 9 ch and then 1 sc in blue. Ch 1 and turn.
Row 2: Work first 2 sc in blue and next 8 sc in rose. Ch 1 and turn.
Rows 3 through 10: Continue moving color line 1 st over, as established, until all sts are in blue. Fasten off.
Part 2: Working with rose along left edge of square just completed, work 1 sc in end of each row as for Row 1. Work Rows 2 through 10 as before. Fasten off. Work Parts 1 and 2 once more. Sew the two pieces just completed together to form one small square (see photo). Sew four small squares together to make one large patterned square (see photo)

Finishing: Sew squares together in a three-by-four arrangement, alternating patterned squares with plain squares. With rose, work 2 rows of sc around entire joined piece, working 3 sc in each corner.

32/ Storm at Sea

Approximate Finished Size: 36 by 46 inches
Experience Needed

The Storm at Sea pattern is a challenging design for both the quilter and the crocheter of the version shown here. Precision-cutting was the element essential to the making of the quilt, which incorporated two shades of blue and white, to capture the illusion of undulating seas, and careful sewing together of the completed squares is crucial to the success of this crocheted lap robe.

Materials:
Dawn Wintuk 100% Du Pont Orlon acrylic, 3½-ounce skeins (knitting worsted weight):
  5 skeins color 301, white
  4 skeins color 312, baby blue
  4 skeins color 318, royal blue
Crochet hook, size H, or size required to crochet to gauge
Yarn needle

Gauge: 7 single crochet = 2 inches; 7 rows = 1 inch

Note: MC (main color) = white; A = baby blue; B = royal blue

Squares: Make 12. With A, ch 4 and join with sl st to form a ring.
Rnd 1: Ch 2, work 15 dc in ring, and join with sl st to second ch of starting ch-2.
Rnd 2: Ch 1, work 3 sc in first st, *1 sc in each of next 3 dc, 3 sc in next st, rep from * around, ending 1 sc in each of next 3 dc; join with sl st to first st. Fasten off.
Rnd 3: Join MC in any center corner sc, work 1 sc in same corner sc, *1 sc in each of next 6 sc — first short row completed — ch 1, turn; skip first sc, 1 sc in each of next 5 sc (leaving last sc unworked), ch 1, turn; skip first sc, 1 sc in each of next 3 sc, ch 1, turn; skip first sc, 1 sc in next sc, ch 1, turn; 1 sl st in end of each of 4 short rows just worked, 1 sc in same st as last sc in first short row, rep from * three times more, working last sc of first short row on third rep in same st as first st of rnd; join with sl st to first st.
Rnd 4: Ch 1, *work 1 sc in end of each of next 4 short rows, work 3 sc in next corner ch-1, 1 sc in each of next 4 sl sts, rep from * three times more, and join with sl st to first st. Fasten off.
Rnd 5: Join B in any corner st, work 1 sc in same corner st, *1 sc in each of next 11 sc — end of first short row — ch 1, turn; skip first sc, 1 sc in each of next 10 sc, ch 1, turn; skip next sc, 1 sc in each of next 8 sc, ch 1, turn; skip first sc, 1 sc in each of next 6 sc, ch 1, turn; skip first sc, 1 sc in each of next 4 sc, ch 1, turn; skip first sc, 1 sc in each of next 2 sc, ch 1, turn; skip 2 sc, 1 sl st in end of each of 6 short rows just worked, rep from * three times more, working last sc of first short row on third rep in same st as first st of rnd, join with sl st to first st.
Rnd 6: Ch 1, *work 1 sc in end of each of next 6 short rows, 3 sc in next corner ch-1, 1 sc in each of next 6 sl sts, rep from * three times more, join with sl st. Fasten off.
Rnd 7: *Join MC in corner st, work 1 sc in same st, 1 sc in each of next 7 sc,

ch 1, turn; skip first sc, work 1 sc in each of next 7 sc, ch 1, turn; continue working in sc for 6 rows more, dec 1 st each row at inner edge only until 1 st remains; ch 1, turn; work 1 sl st in end of each of next 8 short rows, 1 sc in each of next 8 color-B sc on same side of square, ch 1, turn; 1 sc in each of next 7 sc, ch 1, turn; continue working in sc for 6 more rows, dec 1 st each row at inner edge only until 1 st remains. Fasten off.

Rep from * on remaining three sides of square, working last sc of last short row on third rep in same st as first st of rnd. Join with sl st. Fasten off.

Rnd 8: With B, join yarn in ch-1 at tip of right-hand point on any side of square, work 1 sc in same ch-1, 1 sc in each of next 7 sl sts, 1 sc over each of next center 2 sc (inserting hook in st 1 row below previous row to cover MC sc), 1 sc in end of each of next 7 short rows, 1 sc in ch-1 at tip of point, ch 1, turn; skip first sc, 1 sc in each of next 7 sc, skip 2 sc, 1 sc in each of next 7 sc, ch 1, turn; continue to work in sc, skipping first and last sc and center 2 sc of each short row until 2 sts remain. Fasten off. Work in same manner in each angle on each of four sides.

Rnd 9: With A, join yarn in ch-1 at right-hand point in any corner (together with color-B st previously worked), work 1 sc in same ch, 1 sc in edge of each of next 7 short rows, 1 sc in angle between two MC sections (inserting hook into color-B st at corner), 1 sc in each of next 7 short rows, 1 sc in ch-1 at point, ch 1, turn; skip 1 sc, 1 sc in each of next 6 sc, skip 3 sc, 1 sc in each of next 6 sc, ch 1, turn. Continue to work in sc, dec 1 st at beg and end of each row and skipping 2 sts at center until 4 sts remain, ch 1, turn; skip 1 sc, work 1 sc in each of next 2 sts, 1 sl st in next st. Fasten off. Rep in each corner angle.

Corners:

Part 1: Join MC at right edge of any color-A triangle, work 6 sc to center of triangle, ch 1, turn; work in sc, dec 1 st each edge on each row until 2 sts remain. Work 1 sl st in edge of each of next 3 MC short rows, work 6 sc from center of triangle to end of triangle, dec 1 st each edge until 2 sts remain, 1 sl st in next st. Fasten off. Rep on each color-A triangle.

Part 2: Join A in first of 3 sl sts at right-hand point of MC corner just completed, work 1 sc in same sl st, 1 sc in each of next 2 sl sts, 1 sl st in edge of each of first 2 short rows on next MC point, ch 1, turn; skip 2 sl sts, work 1 sc in each of next 3 sc, ch 1, turn; work 1 sc in each of next 3 sc, ending 1 sl st in edge of next short row in MC point. Fasten off.

Finishing: Sew squares together in a three-square-wide by four-square-long arrangement, carefully matching patterns. To make the border, work in sc around joined piece, working 3 sc in each corner, ‸n color sequence as follows: 3 rows B, 2 rows A, 1 row MC, 2 rows A, 3 rows B.

6

Crocheted
Baby Blankets

33/ Yo-Yo

Approximate Finished Size: 31 by 42 inches
No Experience Needed

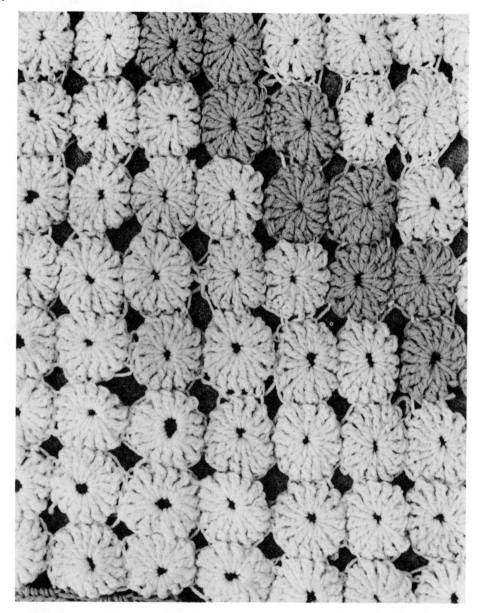

The Yo-yo quilt is an old favorite that is a good "carry-along" project for both quilters and crocheters. All the yo-yos for the crocheted crib blanket you see here were made on bus trips to and from work—only the sewing together of the yo-yos was done at home. Since the yo-yos are attached to one another in only a few places on each side, this blanket is rather delicate; to make it more durable, back it with fabric and tack the yo-yos to the backing.

Materials:
Columbia-Minerva Nantuk, 4-ounce balls (knitting worsted weight):
   3 balls color 5923, baby green
   2 balls color 5987, baby blue
   2 balls color 5972, cornflower
   2 balls color 5921, baby pink
Crochet hook, size I, or size required to crochet to gauge
Yarn needle

Gauge: Each Yo-yo = 2 inches in diameter

Note: Yo-yos are made separately and sewn together later.

Yo-yos: Make 96 in baby green, 68 in baby blue, 54 in cornflower, and 48 in baby pink. Ch 6 and join sl st to form a ring.
Rnd 1: Ch 3, work 15 tr in ring, and join with sl st to third ch of starting ch-3.
Rnd 2: Working through back lps only, work 1 sc in each st around and join with sl st to first st — 16 sc. Fasten off.

Finishing: Folding sc sts to wrong side, sew Yo-yos together with overcast sts taken through top of tr sts and leaving every fourth tr free between joinings. Refer to diagram for placement of Yo-yos.

Border:
Rnd 1: With cornflower, work 1 sc in each of center 3 of 5 unjoined tr on outside edge of any Yo-yo, *ch 3, work 1 sc in each of center 3 unjoined tr on next Yo-yo, rep from * around, working 5 ch in each corner of joined piece instead of 3 ch.
Rnd 2: Work 1 sc in each sc around, working 3 sc in each ch-3 lp and 5 sc in each ch-5 corner lp.
Rnd 3: Work 1 sc in each sc around, working 3 sc in center sc of corner 5 sc. Fasten off.

Optional: You might like to line this blanket with a fabric of your choice.

#33 YO-YO CRIB BLANKET

```
2 3 3 4 4 4 4 4 4 4 4 4 3 3 2
2 2 3 3 4 4 4 4 4 4 4 3 3 2 2
1 2 2 3 3 4 4 4 4 4 3 3 2 2 1
1 1 2 2 3 3 4 4 4 3 3 2 2 1 1
2 1 1 2 2 3 3 3 3 3 2 2 1 1 2
2 2 1 1 2 2 3 3 3 2 2 1 1 2 2
3 2 2 1 1 2 2 2 2 2 1 1 2 2 3
3 3 2 2 1 1 2 2 2 1 1 2 2 3 3
4 3 3 2 2 1 1 1 1 1 2 2 3 3 4
4 4 3 3 2 2 1 1 1 2 2 3 3 4 4
4 3 3 2 2 1 1 1 1 1 2 2 3 3 4
3 3 2 2 1 1 2 2 2 1 1 2 2 3 3
3 2 2 1 1 2 2 2 2 2 1 1 2 2 3
2 2 1 1 2 2 3 3 3 2 2 1 1 2 2
2 1 1 2 2 3 3 3 3 3 2 2 1 1 2
1 1 2 2 3 3 4 4 4 3 3 2 2 1 1
1 2 2 3 3 4 4 4 4 4 3 3 2 2 1
2 2 3 3 4 4 4 4 4 4 4 3 3 2 2
2 3 3 4 4 4 4 4 4 4 4 4 3 3 2
```

Yo-yo Placement

1 = Cornflower

2 = Baby green

3 = Baby blue

4 = Baby pink

34/ Clamshell

Approximate Finished Size: 30 by 40 inches
No Experience Needed

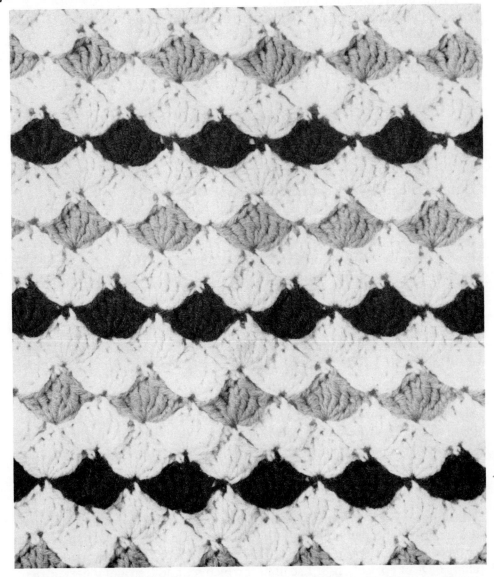

The Clamshell quilt finds its crocheted equivalent in the large scallop pattern used in this afghan for a baby's crib. Shades of peachy pink, rust, and blue make up the "shells," and the finished piece is framed in light blue edged on both sides with navy. If you wish to enlarge the blanket, you can work consecutive borders in various colors around the outer edge.

Materials:

Dawn Wintuk 100% Du Pont Orlon acrylic, 3½-ounce skeins (knitting worsted weight):

  1 skein color 310, apricot
  1 skein color 320, navy blue
  1 skein color 312, baby blue
  1 skein color 360, conch shell

Crochet hook, size I, or size required to crochet to gauge

Yarn needle

Gauge in Pattern Stitch: 2 shells of 7 triple crochet each = 5 inches; 3 rows = 4 inches

Note: To join yarn of a new color at beg of row, make a slip knot on hook, insert hook into designated st, and work first st as specified in directions. Blanket is worked in one piece.

Pattern Stitch: Loosely make a chain of specified length.

Row 1: Work 1 sc in second ch from hook, *skip 3 ch, work 7 tr in next ch (shell made), skip 3 ch, 1 sc in next ch, rep from * across. Fasten off. Do not turn.

Row 2: Return to beg of previous row, join yarn in first sc, ch 3, work 3 tr in same sc, *1 sc in fourth tr of next shell, 1 shell in next sc, rep from * across, ending 1 sc in fourth tr of next shell and 4 tr in last sc. Fasten off. Do not turn.

Row 3: Return to beg of previous row, join yarn in third ch of starting ch-3 of previous row, 1 sc in same ch, *1 shell in next sc, 1 sc in fourth tr of next shell, rep from * across, working last sc into last tr. Rep Rows 2 and 3 for pat st.

Blanket: With apricot, ch 82. Work even in pat st, changing colors as follows: Work first row with apricot and then 1 row each of *apricot, conch shell, apricot, baby blue, navy blue, baby blue; rep from * seven times more, ending 1 row each of apricot, conch shell, apricot, and a second row of apricot.

Finishing: Work 1 row of sc around entire piece, working color over color, using apricot and navy blue as follows: Starting in lower right-hand corner of piece, join apricot in first sc of first row and work 1 sc in same sc, *3 sc along edge of apricot ch-3, 1 sc in next conch sc, and 3 sc along next apricot ch-3. Change to navy blue and work 1 sc in next baby blue sc, 3 sc along next navy blue ch-3, and 1 sc in next baby blue sc. Change to apricot and rep from * across this edge of blanket, working 3 sc in corner at end of last apricot ch-3. Continuing with apricot, work 1 sc in each st across top of piece, 3 sc in corner, next side edge in manner established on first side of piece, 3 sc in next corner, and same number of sc in apricot along bottom edge of piece as on top edge, ending 3 sc in apricot in last corner. Fasten off.

136

Border: Work 1 row of navy blue sc, 4 rows of baby blue sc, and 1 row of navy blue sc around entire piece, working 3 sc in center sc of each corner. Block edges lightly.

35/ Trip Around the World

Approximate Finished Size: 34 by 37 inches
No Experience Needed

Trip Around the World takes its name from the rings of square patches
that surround the center. Another "carry-along" favorite for crocheters,
this baby blanket has been made in rose, lavender, green, and turquoise
on a background of white. To carry out the design for a larger afghan,
continue to alternate "rings" of colored patches with white patches for
as long as you like.

Materials:
Lane Borgosesia Knitaly, 100-gram (3½-ounce) skeins (knitting worsted weight):
   5 skeins color 2428 (white)
   1 skein color 1235 (lavender)
   2 skeins color 1342 (turquoise)
   1 skein color 3657 (green)
   1 skein color 3800 (rose)
Crochet hook, size G, or size required to crochet to gauge
Yarn needle

Gauge: Each square = 2¼ inches

Squares: Make 134 in white, 25 in lavender, 16 in turquoise, 12 in green, 8 in rose. Ch 6 and join with sl st to form a ring.
Rnd 1: Ch 2, work 15 dc in ring, and join with sl st to second ch of starting ch-2.
Rnd 2: Ch 2, work 1 dc in each of next 2 dc, *3 dc in next dc, 1 dc in each of next 3 dc, rep from * twice more, ending 3 dc in last dc; join with sl st to second ch of starting ch-2.
Rnd 3: Ch 1, work 1 sc in each st around with 3 sc in each corner st, and join with sl st to first st. Fasten off.

Finishing: Sew squares together, following diagram for placement of the various colors.

Border: With turquoise and right side of work facing, work in sc around entire joined piece for 2 inches, working 3 sc in each corner on each rnd. Fasten off.

#35 TRIP AROUND THE WORLD

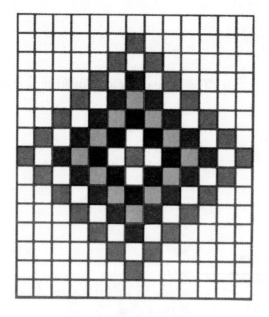

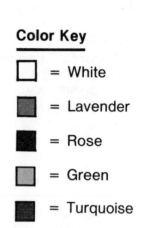

Color Key

☐ = White

▨ = Lavender

■ = Rose

▨ = Green

■ = Turquoise

**Placement Diagram
for Squares**

140

36/ Baby's Flower Garden

Approximate Finished Size: 31 by 40 inches
No Experience Needed

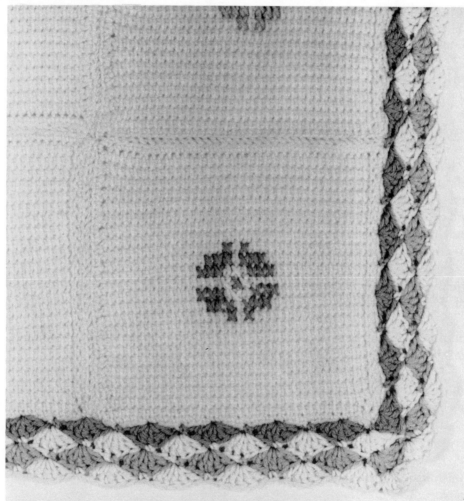

Baby's Flower Garden is based on the many Flower Garden quilts seen throughout the history of quilting. There were many techniques used to create many different types of "flower" quilts. Some boasted flowers pieced in colors contrasting with the background and then appliquéd singly to each square of the quilt; others featured embroidered flowers on solid background squares. For this Baby's Flower Garden, the afghan stitch has been used to make the squares, each of which has then been cross-stitched with a flower in alternating colors. A scalloped border in the colors of the flowers edges this crib blanket.

Materials:
Coats & Clark Red Heart 4-ply hand-knitting yarn, 3½-ounce skeins (knitting worsted weight):

    5 skeins color 230, yellow
    1 skein color 515, dark turquoise
    1 skein color 679, nile green
    1 skein color 584, lavender
    1 skein color 720, young pink

Afghan hook, size K, or size required to crochet to gauge
Crochet hook, size I
Yarn needle

Gauge in Pattern Stitch: 4 stitches = 1 inch; 3 rows = 1 inch

Pattern Stitch: Using afghan hook, make a chain of specified length.
Row 1—first half: Ch 1, insert hook in second ch from hook, yo and draw through, *insert hook in next ch, yo and draw through, rep from * across. *Second half:* Yo and draw through first lp on hook, *yo and draw through 2 lps on hook, rep from * across.
Row 2—first half: Ch 1, skip first vertical bar, *insert hook from right to left under top strand of next vertical bar, yo and draw through, rep from * across, ending by inserting hook under both strands of last vertical bar, yo and draw through. *Second half:* Yo and draw through first lp on hook, *yo and draw through 2 lps on hook, rep from * across.
Rep Row 2 for pat st.

Squares: Make 12. With afghan hook and yellow, ch 36. Work even in pat st for 25 rows. Fasten off.

Finishing: With I hook and yellow, work 1 row of sc around each square, working 3 sc in each corner.

Embroidery: Work cross-stitch embroidery (see Stitch Glossary) as shown on chart, centering one flower on each square and working six squares with a dark turquoise/nile green flower and six with a lavender/young pink flower.

Finishing: Sew the squares together, alternating the flower colors as shown on placement diagram.

Edging:
Rnd 1: With I hook and dark turquoise, join yarn in any corner st and ch 2. Work 4 dc in same corner st (scallop made), *skip 3 sts, 1 sc in next st, skip 3 sts, 5 dc in next st, rep from * around, making sure to place 5 dc in each corner st and ending with skip 3 sc, 1 sc in next st, join with sl st to second ch of starting ch-2. Sl st to center dc of corner scallop. Fasten off.
Rnd 2: Join nile green in center dc of corner scallop, work (1 sc, 5 dc, 1 sc) in same center dc, *5 dc in next sc, 1 sc in center dc of next scallop, rep

from * around, working (1 sc, 5 dc, 1 sc) in center dc of each corner scallop. Join with sl st to first sc. Fasten off.

Rnd 3: With lavender, work as for Rnd 2.

Rnd 4: With young pink, work as for Rnd 2.

#36 BABY'S FLOWER GARDEN

**Cross-Stitch
Embroidery Chart**

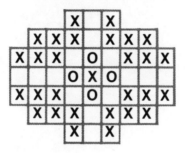

Color Key

X = Dark turquoise
or lavender

O = Nile green or
young pink

☐ = Unworked afghan stitch

Placement Diagram

L	T	L
T	L	T
L	T	L
T	L	T

T = Dark turquoise / nile green

L = Lavender / young pink

Stitch
Glossary

Crochet

Foundation Chain (ch)

Knot a slip loop onto the hook (A). Hold the hook in your right hand and place the long end of the yarn to be used over the index finger of the left hand, under the next two fingers, and loosely around the little finger. *Place the end of the hook under the length of yarn (this is called yarn over — yo), catch the yarn with the hook (B), and pull the yarn through the loop on the shaft of the hook. Repeat this process from the * as many times as specified in the directions.

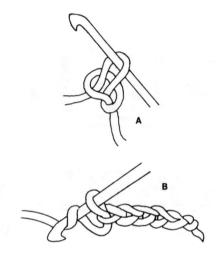

Slip Stitch (sl st)

Insert the hook under the two top strands of the stitch to be worked, place the end of the hook under the yarn (this is called yarn over — yo), catch the yarn with the hook, and pull the yarn through the stitch and the loop on the hook in one motion.

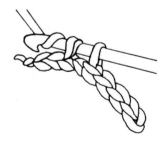

Single Crochet (sc)

Insert the hook under the two top strands of the stitch to be worked, place the end of the hook under the yarn (this is called yarn over — yo), catch the yarn with the hook and pull the yarn through the stitch (two loops are now on the hook); yarn over and pull the yarn through the two loops on the hook.

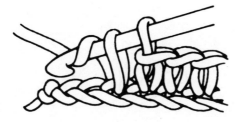

Half Double Crochet (hdc)

Place the end of the hook under the yarn (this is called yarn over — yo), insert the hook under the two top strands of the stitch to be worked; yarn over and pull the yarn through the stitch (three loops are now on the hook); yarn over and pull the yarn through all three loops on the hook in one motion.

Double Crochet (dc)

Place the end of the hook under the yarn (this is called yarn over—yo), insert the hook under the two top strands of the stitch to be worked; yarn over and pull the yarn through the stitch (three loops are now on the hook), yarn over and pull the yarn through the first two loops on the hook; yarn over once more and pull the yarn through the remaining two loops on the hook.

Treble Crochet (tr)

Place the end of the hook under the yarn (this is called yarn over—yo), yarn over once more and insert the hook under the two top strands of the stitch to be worked; yarn over and pull the yarn through the stitch (there are now four loops on the hook); yarn over and pull the yarn through the first two loops on the hook (three loops are now on the hook); yarn over again and pull the yarn through the next two loops on the hook (two loops

are now on the hook); yarn over once more, and pull the yarn through the last two loops on the hook.

To Increase or Decrease (inc or dec)

In this book, the type of decrease or increase to be used, if any, is specified in the directions.

148

Knitting
To Cast On
Make a slip loop on your needle (A) about 2 yards (per 100 stitches to be cast on) from the end of the yarn. Hold the needle in your right hand with the 2-yard end of the yarn closest to you, *make a loop around your left-hand thumb with the 2-yard end and insert the needle from front to back through this loop (B). Wrap the yarn, extending from the skein or ball, under and around the needle (C). Pull the yarn, using the end of the needle, through the loop, and pull the 2-yard end down to tighten it around the needle (D). Repeat from * for the specified number of stitches.

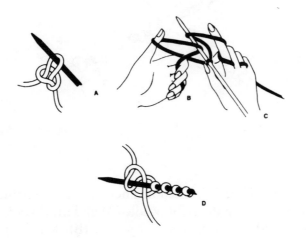

To Knit (k)
Hold the needle with the cast-on stitches in your left hand with the yarn in back of the work, *insert the right needle from left to right through the front of the first stitch, wrap the yarn under and around the right needle to form a loop, pull the tip of the right needle and the loop just made on it through the stitch on the left needle toward the front, and then slip the original stitch off the left needle; repeat from * across the stitches on the left needle.

To Purl (p)

Hold the needle with the cast-on stitches in your left hand with the yarn in front of the work, *insert the right needle from right to left through the front of the first stitch on the left needle, wrap the yarn around the right needle to form a loop, pull the tip of the right needle and the loop just made through the stitch toward the back, and then slip the original stitch off the left needle; repeat from * across the stitches on the left needle.

To Bind Off

Knit or purl, as specified, the first 2 stitches. Then *insert the point of the left needle into the first stitch on the right needle (A) and lift this stitch over the second stitch and off the right needle completely (B). Knit or purl the next stitch. Repeat from * for the number of stitches specified. When all the stitches are to be bound off and you reach the point at which there is only 1 stitch left, cut the yarn and draw the end of the yarn through the stitch.

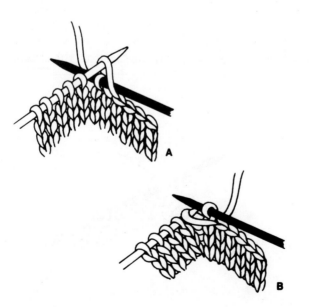

To Increase (inc)

When knitting, knit the stitch in which the increase is to be worked in the usual manner, but do not remove from left needle; work a knit stitch in back loop of same stitch, slip original stitch off left needle. When purling, purl the stitch in which the increase is to be worked in the usual manner, but do not remove from left needle; bring yarn to back of work, work a knit stitch in back loop of same stitch, slip original stitch off left needle.

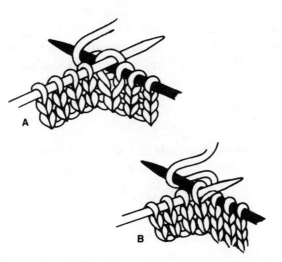

To Decrease (dec) or (k 2 or p 2 tog)

Insert the right needle, either to purl or to knit, as specified, through 2 stitches and work through these 2 stitches together as one.

Slip Stitch (sl st) or (sl 1 as if to p)

Insert the right needle from right to left through the front of the stitch to be slipped and transfer it to the right needle without working it.

Pass Slip Stitch Over (psso)

Lift the slipped stitch on the right needle with the point of the left needle, pass it over the specified number of stitches and the tip of the right needle, and drop it.

Yarn Over (yo)

To work a yarn-over, wrap the yarn around the tip of the right needle once, or as many times as specified, to create an additional loop, or loops, on the right needle, which will be either knitted into on the next row to increase by 1 stitch or dropped to create an elongated stitch.

Embroidery

Cross-Stitch on Afghan Stitch

Each vertical bar of the afghan stitch counts as 1 stitch. Follow the desired diagram for the embroidery design. Join the thread or yarn on the wrong side of the work and bring the needle up through the small space to the lower left of the vertical bar. Then insert the needle down through the space to the upper right of the same vertical bar and then up, to the front, through the space directly below (A). When the specified number of stitches has been worked in this manner, complete each stitch by forming a cross from right to left (B).

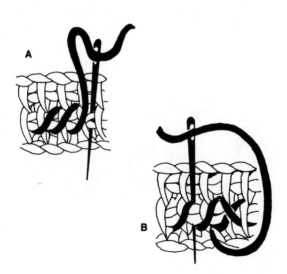

A Portfolio of Traditional Quilt Motifs

Presented here are some of the traditional quilt motifs which inspired the afghans in this book. Mix and match them to create your own designs.

Tree of Life

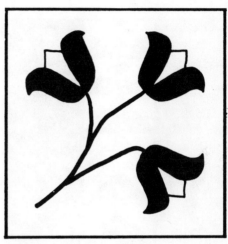

Tulips

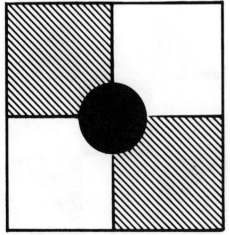

Joseph's Necktie

Goose Tracks

Flying Geese

Log Cabin

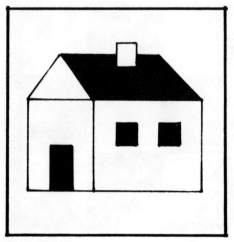

Homestead

Shoofly

Sawtooth

Roman Stripe

Baskets

Indian Hatchet

Double Irish Chain

Cats and Mice

Baby Blocks

Interlocking Squares

Baby's Nine-Patch

Wedding Ring

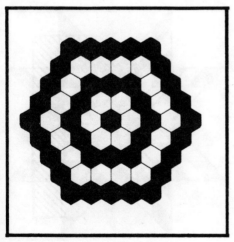

Mosaic

Lone Ring

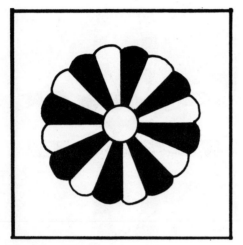

Dresden Plates

Grandmother's Fan

North Carolina Lily

Star of Bethlehem

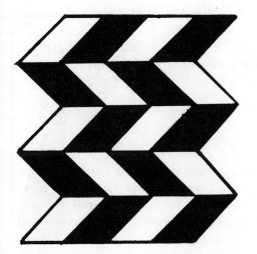

Zigzag

Broken Dishes

Storm at Sea

Trip Around the World

Acknowledgments

Special thanks go to the following professional craftswomen, whose effort and expertise made the creation of these thirty-six afghans possible: Antonia Builes, Peggy Grieg, Michelle Hines, Marie Jourdain, Gail Kahl, Esther Schott, Marilyn Wichnovitz, and last, but not least, the driving force of Bertha Zeltser.

Thanks also go to Maggy Ramsay and Gail Kahl for their careful direction checking.

My gratitude to the Brooklyn Museum for the use of their photographs, showing only a small part of their extensive and beautiful quilt collection, and for the courteous help from their staff.

Sources

The author thanks the following yarn companies for their courteous support and for the opportunity to work with their lovely yarns. If your local yarn shop does not carry the yarn specified in the directions for our afghans, please write to the proper company below for purchasing and ordering information.

American Thread Co., Inc.
High Ridge Park
Stamford, CT 06905

Coats & Clark
Dept. CS
P.O. Box 1010
Toccoa, GA 30577

Columbia-Minerva Corporation
Division of Caron International
P.O. Box 300
Rochelle, IL 61068

Lane Borgosesia
128 Radio Circle
Mount Kisco, NY 10549

Phildar Incorporated
6438 Dawson Boulevard
Norcross, GA 30093

Pingouin Corporation
P.O. Box 100
Jamestown, SC 29453

Reynold's Yarns, Inc.
15 Oser Avenue
Hauppauge, NY 11787